Table of Contents

General principles of criminal law.................................14

   Definition of criminal law and its background...............15

      Background of Criminal Law. 15

      Definition of Crime. 15

      ELEMENTS OF CRIME 16

   Stages of Crime..19

      Conceiving the idea of performing a legally defined harm - 19

      Deliberation -...20

      Intention (Mens Rea) - 20

      Preparation -..21

      Attempt - 21

      Principle of joint liability...25

      Section 34. – Act done in Furtherance of Common intention. 28

      Section 149 - Common object. - 35

      Distinction between "same or similar intention" and "common intention"- 40

Chapter 4. GENERAL EXCEPTIONS (76 to 106) 41

   Introduction..42

      Shivaji v. State of Maharashtra, ...42

      K.M. Nanavati vs State of Maharashtra AIR 1962, ...42

   Defence as to mistake of make of Fact. [76 and 79] 43

Section 76. Act done by a person bound, or by mistake of fact believing himself bound by law. 43

Section 79. 45

Meaning of Mistake - 46

Good faith 49

Ingredients 49

Differences between Section 76 and Section 79. –....49

Section 77. Act of Judge when acting judicially. 50

Section 78. Act done pursuant to the judgment or order of court. 50

Accident. [S. 80] 51

Section 80. Accident in doing a lawful act. - 51

Ingredients 51

Other cases. 55

Accident in an act done with consent 55

Necessity [S. 81] 56

Section 81. Act likely to cause harm but done without criminal intent and to prevent other harm. - 57

Ingredients 57

Act of child, insanity, intoxication (82 to 84) 58

Act of a child 58

Defence of Insanity [84] 61

Intoxication. [85 and 86] 69

Consent (87 to 92) 74

Section 87. Act not intended and not known to be likely to cause death or grievous hurt, done by consent. – 74

Section 88. Act not intended to cause death, done by consent in good faith for person's benefit. - – 75

Section 89. Act done in good faith for the benefit of child or insane person by consent of guardian. – 76

Section 90. Consent known to be given under fear or misconception. 77

Section 91. Exclusion of acts which are offences independently of harm caused. – 79

Section 92. Act done in good faith for the benefit of a person without consent. – 79

Other Defences and Provisions. [93 to 95] 81

Section 93. Communication made in good faith. – 81

Section 94. Act to which a person is compelled by threats. – 81

Section 95. Act causing slight harm. – [De minimis non Curat lex] 83

Section 95 and Adulteration Act. – 84

THE RIGHT OF PRIVATE DEFENCE (96 to 106) 84

Restrictions on right to private defence 87

Chapter 5. - of Abetment (107 to 120) 109

Section 107. Abetment of a thing. – 109

Ingredients 110

Whether attempt to abetment is punishable? – 111

Section 108. Abettor. - 112

Ingredients. – 112

S. 109 - Act Abetted is committed 113

Ingredients 114

S. 110 – Act done with different intention. 115

S. 111 - Different act done 115

S. 112- Cumulative punishment for act abetted and act done. 116

S. 113 Liability for the act different for intended. 117

Section 114. Abettor present when offence is committed. – 117

Ingredients 118

Section 115. Abetment of offence punishable with death or imprisonment for life – 118

Section. 116. Abetment of offence punishable with imprisonment. – 119

Section 117. Abetting commission of offence by the public or more than ten persons. – 120

Section 118. Concealing design to commit offence punishable with death or imprisonment for life. – 121

Section 119. Public Servant concealing design to commit offence which it is his duty to prevent. – 121

Chapter 5A. Criminal conspiracy (120A, 120B.) 122

Introduction – 122

Section 120A. Definition of criminal conspiracy. – 123

120B- Punishment. – 123

Ingredients of Criminal Conspiracy 124

Chapter 6 – of Offences related to State (121 to 130)......125

   SEDITION...125

      Ingredients 126

Chapter 7 – Offence Related to Army, Navy and Airforce. (131 to 140)..127

Chapter 8 - of offences against the public tranquility (140 to 160) 127

   Section 141. Unlawful assembly. 127

      Who will be treated as a member of unlawful assembly? - 129

   Section 146. Rioting –...129

Chapter 9 - OF OFFENCES BY OR RELATING TO PUBLIC SERVANTS [161 to 171] 130

Chapter 16 - OF OFFENCES AFFECTING THE HUMAN BODY (299 to 377) 131

   Section 299. Culpable Homicide. – 131

      Ingredients. - 131

      THREE Explanations provided by section 299. 132

      Whoever causes death? -..133

      By doing an act. -..133

      Intention. -...133

      With the knowledge by act to cause death. -............136

      Death of a human being is caused - 137

   MURDER [300 and 302] 137

      No intention to commit crime. - 138

Significance of motive. - 138

Exceptions - Situations where Culpable Homicide does not amount to Murder 139

Punishment for murder (section 302). 144

Ingredients 144

Distinction between Section 299 and Section 300 - 152

Murder (When Culpable Homicide amounts to Murder) 153

Illustrations - 153

Section 301. Culpable homicide by causing death of person other than person whose death was intended. – 157

Section 303. Murder committed by life convict. (Repealed.) 157

Section 304-A. Causing death by negligence. – 158

Section 304B. Dowry Death - 158

Explanation. – 158

Dowry death. - 159

Conviction of accused. - 160

Conviction for murder. - 161

Case does not fall within the four corners of Section 304 B of IPC. - 161

Sustainability of conviction. - 162

Conviction of appellant. - 163

Abetment of suicide 163

Section 305. Abetment of suicide of child or insane person. – 163

Section 306. Abetment of suicide. – 164

Section 307. Attempt to murder - 164

    Comment - 164

    Example. – 165

    Is Injury necessary. 165

    Whether act committed must be capable of causing death. 166

    Penultimate Act not necessary 166

Section 308. Attempt to commit culpable homicide. - 166

Section 309. -Attempt to commit suicide - 167

    Section 307, 308, 309 and Section 511 167

Section 312. Causing miscarriage. – 169

Hurt and Grievous Hurt 169

    Section 319 - Hurt 169

    Grievous Hurt (320) 170

    Section 330. Voluntarily causing hurt to extort confession or to compel restoration of property. - 173

Wrongful restraint and wrongful confinement. 174

    Section 339. Wrongful restraint – 174

    Section 340. Wrongful confinement - 175

    Distinction between wrongful restraint and wrongful confinement. 175

Assault and Criminal Force (349 to 358) 176

    Section 349. Force. – 176

    Section 350. Criminal Force. - 177

Section 351. Assault. – 178

Distinction between assault and criminal force is as follows: 179

Kidnapping and Abduction 179

Kidnapping 179

Section 363. Punishment. – 182

Abduction (362) 185

Differences among Kidnapping from India, Kidnapping from lawful guardian, and Abduction - 186

Distinction between abduction and kidnapping 188

Section 364. Kidnapping or abduction in order to murder. - 189

Section 364A. Kidnapping for ransom, etc. 190

Section 366. Kidnapping, abducting or inducing woman to compel her to marriage, etc. - 190

Section 366A - Procuration of minor girl. – 191

Section 368-B. Importation of girl from foreign country. - 191

SEXUAL OFFENCES 191

Section 375. Rape. – 191

(A) Sexual intercourse by a man with a woman. 193

(B) The sexual intercourse must be under circumstances falling under any of the seven clauses of Section 375. 194

Explanation. - 196

Exception. - 196

Section 376. Punishment for rape – 197

376A. Punishment for causing death or resulting in persistent vegetative state of victim. – 199

376B. Sexual intercourse by husband upon his wife during separation. - 200

376C. Sexual intercourse by a person in authority. -200

376D. Gang Rape. -..202

376E. Punishment for repeat offenders. -................202

of Unnatural Offences (377) 207

Difference between rape and adultery. 208

Chapter 17. of Offences Against Property (378 to 462)...209

Theft, Robbery and Dacoity 209

Theft (378 to 382) 209

Extortion (383) 218

Differences between theft and extortion. 223

ROBBERY AND DACOITY 223

Robbery 223

Dacoity..229

Distinction between Robbery and Dacoity 231

Criminal MISAPPROPRIATION OF PROPERTY................232

Criminal Breach of trust. 236

Section 405. Criminal breach of trust. -..................236

OF CHEATNG 240

Section 415. Cheating. – 240

Section 416. Cheating by personation. -................243

Section 419. Punishment. 244

Section 420. Cheating and dishonestly inducing delivery of property. - 244

MISCHIEF 245

    Section 425. Mischief. - 245

    Section 426. Punishment for mischief. - 246

CRMINAL TRESPASS 247

    Section 441. Criminal trespass. - 247

    Section 442. House-trespass. - 249

    Section 443. Lurking house-trespass. - 250

    Section 444. Lurking house-trespass by night. - 250

    Section 445. Housebreaking. - 250

Chapter 18 - OF OFFENCES RELATING TO DOCUMENTS AND TO PROPERTY MARKS [463 to 489] 252

    Section 463. Forgery. - 252

    Section 464. -Making a false document. - 252

        Illustrations 253

        Explanation 1 255

        Illustrations 255

        Illustration 257

    Section 465. Punishment for forgery. - 257

        INGREDIENTS OF FORGERY 257

        Muhammad Saeed Khan case 258

    Section 467. Forgery of valuable security, will, etc. - 261

    Section 468. Forgery for purpose of cheating. - 261

Section 469 Forgery for purpose of harming reputation. – 262

Section 470. Forged document - 262

Section 471. Using as genuine a forged document. - ...262

ESSENTIAL INGREDIENTS..262

Abdul Ghafur, ...263

Mulai Singh, ...263

M.M. Trivedi v. State of M.P., ...263

Section 477A: Ratification of accounts. – 263

Chapter 19. Of the Criminal Breach of Contracts of Service (490 to 492) 265

CHAPTER 20 - OF OFFENCES RELATING TO MARRIAGE [493 to 498]..265

Section 494. Marrying again during the lifetime of husband or wife. – 266

Section 496. Marriage ceremony fraudulently gone through without lawful marriage. - 270

ESSENTIAL INGREDIENTS..270

Section 497: Adultery. – 271

Section 498: Enticing or taking away or detaining with criminal intent a married woman. – 272

CHAPTER 20A - OF CRUELTY BY HUSBAND OR RELATIVES OF HUSBAND [498A] 273

Section 498A. - CRUELTY BY HUSBAND OR RELATIVES OF HUSBAND. 274

Punishment of husband. - 275

In Sarla Prabhakar Waghmare v. State of Maharashtra,275

In Tapan Pal v. State of W.B., ...276

In Bathala Subbarayudu v. State of A.P., ...276

In Balbir Singh v. State of Punjab, ...277

CHAPTER 21 - OF DEFAMATION [499 to 502]...................277

Section 499. Defamation. – 277

EXCEPTIONS..278

Section 500. Punishment for defamation. - 280

ESSENTIAL INGREDIENTS..280

Section 501. Printing or engraving matter known to be defamatory. - 283

Section 502. Sale of printed or engraved substance containing defamatory matter. - 284

CHAPTER 22 - OF CRIMINAL INTIMIDATION, INSULT AND ANNOYANCE [503 to 511] 284

Section 503: Criminal Intimidation. – 284

ESSENTIAL INGREDIENTS..284

Section 506. Punishment for criminal intimidation. –285

Section 504. -Intentional insult with intent to provoke breach of the peace. - 286

ESSENTIAL INGREDIENTS..286

Section 505. -Statements conducing to public mischief. –286

Exception. - 288

Section 507. Criminal intimidation by an anonymous communication. - 288

Section 509. Word, gesture or act intended to insult the modesty of a woman. –..289

    ESSENTIAL INGREDIENTS..289

Section 510: Misconduct in public by a drunken person. –290

    ESSENTIAL INGREDIENTS..290

CHAPTER 23 - OF ATTEMPTS TO COMMIT OFFENCES 290

PROBLEMS AND SOLUTIONS..293

    1. 293
    2. 294
    3. 294
    4. 295
    5. 295
    6. 296
    7. 296
    8. 297
    9. 297
    10. 298
    11. 298
    12. 298
    13. 299
    14. 299
    15. 300
    16. 300
    17. 301

18. 301
19. 301
20. 302
21. 303
22. 303
23. 304

GENERAL PRINCIPLES OF CRIMINAL LAW

Definition of criminal law and its background

Background of Criminal Law.

The origin of crime is as old as society itself. An act punishable by law as forbidden by statute or injurious to public welfare is crime. There is no concept of criminal law in an uncivilized society. In India, criminal jurisprudence came into existence from the time of Manu. Manu has categorised crime as assault, theft, robbery cheat, false evidence, adultery and rape, murder, etc. For those crimes penal system of our Indian society was caste based. Punishment was not according to the offence, but it was on the basis of caste. Brahmin could not be hanged although he had committed the offence of murder.

The Muslim law of jurisprudence was also on the basis of religion. Evidence of non-Muslim was not admissible against Muslim. Mr. Lord Macaulay is modern Manu of India. Criminal and social engineering was started first at that time.

Definition of Crime.

Various authors have defined crime as follows:

According to **Austin** - "A wrong which is pursued at the discretion of the injured party and his representatives is a civil injury, a wrong pursued by the sovereign or his subordinate is a crime."

According to **ketone** - "A crime would seem to be any undesirable act which the state finds it most convenient to correct by the institution of proceedings for the infliction of a penalty, instead of leaving the remedy to the discretion of some injured person."

According to **Bentham** - "Offences are whatever the legislature has prohibited for good or bad reasons."

According to **Black Stone** - "Crime is an act in violation of public law. Crime is an act done in violation of public rights and duties."

Paton points out about crime as - "the normal marks of an aimed are that the state has power to control the procedure to remit the penalty or to inflict the punishment."

Thus, from the above definitions we find that it is very difficult to suggest a suitable definition of crime. Modern approach or criminal law is that there are certain standards of behaviour of moral principles which society requires to be observed and the breach of them is an offence not merely against the person who is injured hut against society as a whole.

First Indian law commission was established in 1834 under the charter act of 1833 to investigate into the jurisdiction, powers, general rules of the courts and police establishment and law operation in the British India and make reports thereon and suggest alteration, modification with due respect of caste, race, religion, etc. About customs operated as a law in that time in different parts of the country. The principle of our criminal law is uniformity when you have it diversity when you must have it, but in all cases certainty.

ELEMENTS OF CRIME

To constitute crime mental elements are necessary.
Mental elements are—

- Intention,
- motive,
- mens rea,
- knowledge,
- mistake of fact,
- mistake of law,
- innocence which plays a significant role in criminal law.

INTENTION

Intention is the **purpose or design** with which an act is done. The intention is the aim of the act, of which the motive is the spring. The purpose or design of doing an act forbidden by law is generally known as intention.

According to Stephen - Intention is an operation of the will directing an overt act. Motive is the feeling which prompts the operation of the will the ulterior object of the person willing."

MOTIVE

Motive is the object for which crime takes place. If a man knows that a certain consequence will follow from his act or omission, it must be presumed in law that he intended to do that act. The motive for an act is not a sufficient test to determine its criminal character. Whether there is direct evidence to show that crime has been committed by the accused and acts are sufficient to disclose the intention of the actor in those cases the motive becomes immaterial. Absence of the motive is a factor which may be considered in determining the guilt of the accused. Thus, motive also play a very significant role to constitute a crime.

MENS REAI

Mental element of crime is known as mens rea. It is one of the main principles of English Criminal Law. The liability to conviction of an individual depends not only on his having done some outward acts which the law forbids, but on his having done them in a certain frame of mind or with a certain will, which are known as mental elements in criminal responsibility. Therefore, an act in order to be a crime must be committed with a guilty mind- **Actus non facit reum nisi mens sit rea** is a well settled legal maxim which means that act alone did not make a man guilty unless his intentions were so. The basic requirement of the principle of mens rea is that accused must have been aware of all those elements in his act which make it the crime with which he is charged. That means he must have intended the actus reus or have been reckless whether he caused actus reus or not. It is not necessary that he must know that the act which he is going to commit is a crime.

In the earliest, time the trials were held on fundamental presumption that a man must almost in every case be deemed to have intended to do what he had done. In the ancient times, in English Criminal Law, the principles of strict liability for in those days the distinction between crime and tort was not clearly drawn and punishment in those days mainly consisted of money compensation to the person wronged. Therefore, the mental attitude of a person was an irrelevant consideration in so far as the trial and punishment were concerned. Later on, bodily punishment came as a substitute of the payment of damages. Then the importance of mens rea to constitute a crime was realized.

The first systematic treatment of mens rea was provided by Hale.

According to Hale—"The penal liability was based on two great faculties understanding and liberty of will. No one incurs penal liability for doing an act without intention of any bodily harm to any person. Malice in fact, has become a deliberate intention of doing some corporal wrong to the person Of another. Thus, mens rea consist of two elements, first is the intent to do an act and record a knowledge of the circumstances that makes that act a criminal offence: In the case of State of Maharashtra v. Mayor Hans George, it was discussed by the Supreme Court that only act of a person does not constitute a crime unless his intention is not criminal. The mens rea has certain exceptions, for example, public nuisance, strict liability, petty offences, etc.

Stages of Crime

In general, an offence passes through the following stages -

Conceiving the idea of performing a legally defined harm -

It is immaterial whether the person conceiving such an idea knows that it is illegal to perform it. At this stage, there is no action taken to harm anybody and it is not a crime to merely think of doing harmful activity because the person thinking it may not even want to actually do it. For example, merely thinking killing 1000s of people instantaneously, is not a crime.

Deliberation -

At this stage, a person consolidates his devious ideas and identifies ways of doing it. Again, there is no action taken and there is no harm done to anybody nor is there any intention to cause injury to anybody. It is still in the thinking stage and is not a crime. For example, merely thinking about how to build a device that can kill 1000s of people instantaneously, is not a crime.

From a legal standpoint the above two stages are inconsequential because man being a thoughtful animal, he thinks about innumerable things without any material result.

Intention (Mens Rea) -

This stage is a significant progress from mere deliberation towards actual commission of the crime. At this stage, the person has made up his mind to actually implement or execute his devious plans. There is an intention to cause harm, but he hasn't yet taken any action that manifests his intention. Further, there is no way to prove an intention because even devil can't read a human mind. Thus, this is not considered a crime. For example, intention to kill anyone is not a crime in itself. However, it is an essential ingredient of crime because without intention to cause harm, there can be no crime. On the other hand, even a thoughtless act, without any deliberation, can be a crime if there is an intention to cause harm.

Preparation -

As this stage, the intention to cause harms starts manifesting itself in the form of physical actions. Preparation consists of arranging or building things that are needed to commit the crime. For example, purchasing poison. However, it is possible for the person to abandon his course of action at this stage without causing any harm to anyone. In general, preparation is not considered a crime because it cannot be proved beyond doubt the goal of the preparation. For example, purchasing knife with an intention to kill someone is not a crime because it cannot be determined whether the knife was bought to kill someone or to chop vegetables.

However, there are certain exceptions where even preparation for committing an offence is crime. These are -

Sec 122 - Collecting arms with an intention of waging war against the Govt. of India.

Sec 126 - Preparing to commit depredation on territories of any power in alliance or at peace with the Govt. of India.

Sec 235 - Counterfeiting operations for currency.

Sec 399 - Preparation to commit dacoity.

Attempt -

This stage is attained by performing physical actions that, if left unstopped, cause or are bound to cause injury to someone. The actions clearly show that the person has absolutely no intention to abandon his plan and if the person is left unrestricted, he will complete the commission of the crime. Since the intention of the person can be determined without doubt from his actions, an attempt to commit a crime is considered a crime because if left unpunished, crime is bound to happen, and prevention of crime is equally important for a healthy society.

Actual commission of the offence - This is the final stage where the crime is actually done.

Distinction between Preparation and Attempt

There is a very fine line between preparation and attempt. While IPC does not define either of them, it is very important to distinguish between them because attempt is a crime, but preparation is not. Both, Preparation and Attempt are physical manifestations of the criminal intention. But attempt goes a lot forward than preparation towards the actual happening of crime. While in Preparation, there is a possibility that the person may abandon his plan, but attempt leaves no room for that. For example, keeping a pistol in pocket and looking for the enemy to kill is a preparation because one can abandon the plan anytime, but taking out the piston and pulling the trigger is attempt because it leaves no room for turning back. Thus, in general, Preparation involves collecting material, resources, and planning for committing an act while attempt signifies a direct movement towards commission after the preparations are made.

Ordinarily, to constitute an attempt the following elements are needed -

1. mens rea to commit the crime
2. ant act which constitutes the actus reus of a criminal attempt
3. failure in accomplishment

In the case of **R vs Cheeseman 1862, Lord Blackburn** identified a key difference between the two. He says that if the actual transaction has commenced which would have ended in the crime if not interrupted, there is clearly an attempt to commit the crime.

However, this is not the only criteria for determining an attempt. The following are four tests that come in handy in distinguishing between the two -

1. Last Step Test or Proximity Rule
2. As per this test, anything short of last step is preparation and not attempt. This is because as long as there is a step remaining for completion of the crime, the person can abandon it. For example, A obtains poison to kill B and mixes it with food

that B is supposed to eat. But he has not yet given the food to B. Thus, it is still preparation. As soon as he keeps the food on the table from where B eats every day, the last step is done, and it becomes an attempt.

3. In the case of **R vs Riyasat Ali 1881**, the accused gave orders to print forms that looked like they were from Bengal Coal Company. He proofread the samples two times and gave orders for correction as well so that they would appear exactly as forms of the said company. At this time, he was arrested for attempt to make false document under section 464. However, it was held that it was not an attempt because the name of the company and the seal were not put on the forms and until that was done, the forgery would not be complete.

4. In the case of **Abhayanand Mishra vs State of Bihar AIR 1961**, A applied to the Patna University for MA exam, and he supplied documents proving that he was a graduate and was working as a headmaster of a school. Later on, it was found that the documents were fake. It was held that it was an attempt to cheat because he had done everything towards achieving his goal.

5. Indispensable Element Test or Theory of Impossibility

6. As per this test, all of indispensable elements must be present to equal attempt. For example, a person has the gun to kill but he forgot the bullets. In this case, it would not be an attempt. Further, he goes to place where victim should be but is not then he is not guilty of attempt under this test. In other words, if there is something a person needs to commit the crime, but it is not present, then there is not an attempt. This test has generated a lot of controversy ever since it was laid in the case of **Queen vs Collins**, where it was held that a pickpocket was not guilty of attempt even when he put his hand into the pocket of

someone with an intention to steal but did not find anything. Similarly, in the case of **R vs Mc Pherson 1857**, the accused was held not guilty of attempting to break into a building and steal goods because the goods were not there.

7. However, these cases were overruled in **R vs King 1892**, where the accused was convicted for attempting to steal from the hand bag of a woman although there was nothing in the bag. Illustration (b) of section 511 is based on this decision.

8. But For Interruption Test

9. If the action proves that the person would have gone through with the plan if not for the interruption such as arrest, then it is an attempt. For example, a person points a gun at another and is about to pull the trigger. He is overpowered and was stopped from pulling the trigger. This shows that if he had not been interrupted, he would have committed the crime and he is thus guilty of attempt even though the last step of the crime has not been performed.

10. Unequivocally Test or On the job Theory

11. If a person does something that shows his commitment to follow through and commit the crime then it is an attempt. For example, in the case of **State of Maharashtra vs Mohd. Yakub 1980**, three persons were found with a truck loaded with silver near the sea dock. Further, the sound of engine of a mechanized boat was heard from a nearby creek. They were convicted of attempting to smuggle silver. **J Sarkaria** observed that what constitutes at attempt is a mixed question of law and the facts of a case. Attempt is done when the culprit takes deliberate and overt steps that show an unequivocal intention to commit the offence even if the step is not the penultimate one.

Principle of joint liability

There are certain provisions under which the liability of a person committing a crime is joint with some other persons. Normally, a person may be a participant in a crime in the following four ways -
(1) When he himself commits a crime;
(2) When he shares in the commission of it;
(3) when he with a view to the commission of crime sets some third agency to work that is he makes some third party his own agent for committing the crime; and
(4) When he helps the offender, after the commission of the crime, in screening him from justice.
Section 34 enunciates the principle of joint liability.

In **Sewa Ram v. State of U.P.,** The Supreme Court held that section 34 has been enacted on principle of joint liability in doing of a criminal act. Section is only rule of evidence and does not create substantive offence. Distinctive feature of section 34 is element of participation in action.

Section 34, IPC Embodies the principle of joint liability in the doing of a criminal act and essence of that liability is the existence of common intention. Common intention implies acting in concert and existence of a pre-arranged plan which is to be proved or inferred either from the conduct of the accused persons or from attendant circumstances. To invoke section 34, IPC, It must be established that the criminal act was done by more than one person in furtherance of common intention of all. It must, therefore, be proved that: -

    (1) There was common intention on the part of several persons to commit a particular crime, and
    (2) The crime was actually committed by them in furtherance of that common intention.

Common intention implies prearranged plan. -

Under section 34, a pre-concert in the sense of a distinct previous plan is not necessary to be proved. The essence of liability under section 34, IPC Is conscious mind of persons participating in the criminal action to bring about a particular result. The question whether there was any common intention or not depends upon inference to be drawn from the proven facts and circumstances of such case. The totality of the circumstances must be taken into consideration in arriving at the conclusion whether the accused had a common intention to commit an offence with which they could be convicted.

Rule of criminal liability. -

Ordinary rule of criminal liability is that a person who actually commits an offence has the primary responsibility to suffer punishment for the - same. Section 34, IPC, However, within the ambit of penal liability even those persons(s) who have not actually committed crime but there a common intention animating

The accused leading to the doings of a criminal act in furtherance of such intention. Thus, to attract section 34, which in fact enumerates one of the principles of constructive liability, two conditions must be satisfied

(1) There must be common intention to commit a criminal act; and

(2) There must be participation by all the persons in doing such act in furtherance of that in tension.

Constructive liability. -

Facts and circumstances of the case show that the attack was not a premeditated one nor was there a prior concert. Initially settlement talks were on, and fight started only when the accused party was informed by their person that Anand was cut by complainant party and thus the incident arose suddenly. No doubt, common intention could develop even at the spur of the moment; but in the present case, the way the occurrence took place as depicted by the prosecution, there could not have been common intention between the accused. The totality of the circumstances must be taken into consideration in order to arrive at a conclusion that the appellant had a common intention to commit the offence under which they were convicted. The appellants were not armed and admittedly they are said to have removed sticks from the bullock cart standing nearby and not the exhortation by accused no.1 - Giri, the appellants have attacked Ramesh. There may be similar intention in the minds of the assailants to attack; but it cannot be said that the appellants have acted in furtherance of common intention to attract constructive liability under section 34 IPC.

Section 34. – Act done in Furtherance of Common intention.

When a criminal act is done by several persons, in furtherance of common intention of all, each of such persons is liable for that act in the same manner as if it were done by him alone.

Ingredients. -

There should be following ingredients to constitute joint liability under
Section 34, Indian penal code -

    (1) Some **criminal act** is done;

    (2) A criminal act was done by **more than one person**;

    (3) A criminal act was done by such persons in furtherance of the common intention of all of them;

    (4) The common intention in the sense of **prearranged plan between such persons;**

(5) **Participation in some manner** in the act constituting the offence by the persons sought to be prosecuted; and

(6) **Physical presence** at the time of the commission of the crime of all the persons, but the physical <u>presence of all is not necessary</u> in some cases.

In **State of M.P. v. Deshraj,** it was held that section 34 of the penal code has been enacted on the principle of joint liability in the doing of a criminal act.

Criminal act. –

The word "criminal act" used in this section means the unity of criminal behaviour which results in something for which an individual would be punishable if it were all done by himself alone in an offence. The criminal act must necessarily be done by more than one person. Section 34 does not refer to individual acts where a crime is committed by a group of persons.

In Furtherance of common intention. -

As initially enacted, the words "**in furtherance of the common intention of all**" were not part of section 34 but came to be introduced by section 1 of Act no. 27 of 1970. The reason for inserting such amendment was the observations made by Sir Barnes Peacock, C.J., in Queen v. Gora Chand, holding that mere presence of a person at the scene of crime would not be sufficient to hold him liable to be implicated under section 34, IPC as it stood then, unless such presence was an act in furtherance of a common design.

Pre-concert in the sense of a distinct previous plane –

Under Section 34, IPC, a pre-concert in the sense of a distinct previous plan is not necessary to be proved. The common intention to bring about a particular result may well develop on the spot as between a number of persons, with reference to the facts of the case and circumstances of the situation. The question whether there was any common intention or not depends upon the inference to be drawn from the proving facts and circumstances of each case. The totality of the circumstances must be taken into consideration in arriving at the conclusion whether the accused had a common intention to commit an offence with which they could be convicted.

Meeting of Mind is essential. -

It is now well settled that a conspiracy is ordinarily hatched in secrecy. The Court for the purpose of arriving at a finding as to whether the said offence has been committed or not may take into consideration the circumstantial evidence. However, while doing so, it must be borne in mind that meeting of the mind is essential; mere knowledge or discussion would not be sufficient. Yet, the prosecution has failed to prove the evidence which establishes any prior meeting of mind of the accused. The prosecution merely proved that all the accused were present in Delhi on the date of occurrence and that the alleged motorbike and the car used in the incident belonged to respondent No. 2, Om Prakash Srivastava. The High Court rightly dismissed this argument, as the involvement of the said vehicles in the commission of the crime were never proved. Neither any prior meetings of mind of the accused was proved, nor was any action, individually or in concert, proved against any of the accused. Needless to say, that the entire foundation of the prosecution story was never established.

The essence of liability. -

Under section 34 the essence of liability is to be found in the existence of a common intention animating the accused leading to the doings of a criminal act in furtherance of such intention. As a result of the application of principles enunciated in section 34, when an accused is convicted under Section 302 read with Section 34, in law it means that the accused is liable for the act which caused the death of the deceased in the same manner as if it was done by him alone. The provision is intended to meet a case in which it may be difficult to distinguish between acts of individual members of a party who act in furtherance of the common intention of all or to prove exactly what part was taken by each of them.

Pulla Reddy and others v. State of Andhra Pradesh.

It was observed that section 34 is applicable even if no injury has been caused by the particular accused himself. For applying section 34, it is not necessary to show some overt act on the part of the accused. This decision has been followed in Anil Sharma and others v. the State of Jharkhand.

Common intention. –

The word "common intention" implies a pre-arranged plan, prior meeting of minds, and prior consultation in between all the persons constituting the group. A desire to commit a criminal act without any contemplation of the consequences. The common intention comes into being prior to the commission of the act in point of time. But there need not be a long interval of time between the formation of the common intention and the doing of the act. The essence of the liability is to be found in the existence of a common intention emanating the accused leading to the doings of a criminal act in furtherance of such intention. It must be shown that the criminal act complained against was done by one of the accused persons in furtherance of common intention of all, if this is shown, then liability for the crime may be imposed on any one of the persons in the same manner as if the act were done by him alone. Common intention does not mean similar or same intention of several persons. To constitute common intention, it is necessary that intention of each one of them be known to the rest of them and shared by them. In order to understand the principle of common intention some important cases are useful which are as follows: -

Barendra Kumar Ghosh v. Emperor,

In case of **Barendra Kumar Ghosh v. Emperor,** the appellant was charged under Section 302/34 of Indian Penal Code. The facts of this case were: on August 3 of 1923, sub-postmaster of Shankar Tola post office was counting money in the back room. Several persons appeared at the door which opened into the room from the courtyard of the office. They demanded the sub-postmaster to give up the money and immediately afterwards fired pistols at him. The sub-postmaster died immediately. The assailants fled away in different directions without taking the money, but one of them Barendra Kumar Ghosh was chased by post office assistants. Although he fired several rounds with his pistol but was caught with a pistol in his hand. Barendra Kumar Ghosh was prosecuted and tried for murder under Section 302 of Indian Penal Code read with Section 34 of the Indian Penal Code. It was held by the Privy Council that all ingredients of Section 34 are satisfied and liability of Barendra Ghosh was common in this case.

Mahboob Shah v. Emperor,

Another well-known case is **Mahboob Shah v. Emperor**, under which common intention was discussed. The Privy Council held that in the instant case there was no evidence and there were no circumstances from which it could be inferred that Mahboob Shah, the appellant acted in concert with Wali Shah in pursuance of a pre plan when former along with later rushed to rescue of Ghulam Quasim. The two had the same intention, namely, the intention to rescue Quasim Shah if need be, by the use of the guns and that in carrying out this intention Mahboob Shah picked out Hamidullah and Wali Shah, the deceased (Allahdad) for dealing. But where in the evidence of common intention to commit the criminal act complained against in furtherance of common intention there was no case for conviction of appellant for murder. There was no evidence that appellant and Wali Shah ever entered into a premeditated concert to bring about the murder of Wali Shah in carrying out their intention to rescue the Quasim Shah.

Sewer Ram v. State of U.P.,

In Sewer Ram v. State of U.P., it was held by the Supreme Court that direct proof of common intention is seldom available. It can only be inferred from circumstances appearing from proved facts.

The true concept of Section 34 is that if two or more persons intentionally do an act jointly, position in law is just the same as if each of them has done it individually by himself.

Sustainability of conviction. - in the present case, there is concurrent findings of conviction of the appellant by the Sessions Court and the High Court on the basis of the statement of eyewitness (PW2) and its corroboration by the medical evidence. In view of the submissions made by the learned counsel for both parties, we find that since the acquittal of all caucused has become final, the conviction of the appellant under Section 34 becomes unsustainable.

Necessary conditions for applicability of section. –

VIRENDRA SINGH V. STATE OF MADHYA PRADESH,
It was held that vicarious liability under Section 34 of IPC can arise only when two conditions are fulfilled, i.e., the mental element or the intention to commit the criminal act conjointly with another and the other is the actual participation in one form or the other in the commission of the crime.

The common intention postulates the existence of a pre-arranged plan implying a prior meeting of the minds. It is the intention to commit the crime that the accused can be convicted only if such an intention has been shared by all the accused. Thus, the dominant feature of Section 34 of IPC is the element of intention and Participation in the act. This participation need not in all cases be by physical presence. Common intention implies acting in concert.

Section 34 of IPC does not create any distinct offence but lays down the principle of constructive liability. Section 34 postulates that the act must have been done in furtherance of common intention.

Section 149 - Common object. -

Section 149 provides that if an offence is committed by any member of an unlawful assembly in prosecution of the common object of the assembly, or such as the members of that assembly knew to be likely to be committed in prosecution of that object every person who at the time of the committing of that offence is a member of the same assembly is guilty of that offence.

INGREDIENTS

1. Some offence must be committed by any member of an unlawful assembly.
2. Such offence must have been committed in prosecution of common object of the assembly or must be such as a member of the assembly knew to be likely to be committed.

Mahmood v. State of U.P.,

It was held by Supreme Court that once it is established that a person was a member of unlawful assembly, prosecution need not establish any specific overt act to any of the accused for fastening of liability with the aid of Section 149,

In Raj Nath v. State of U.P.,

the Apex Court held that proof of some overt act by person constituting it, not necessary to hold him to be member of unlawful assembly.

"in prosecution of common object" -
The words "in prosecution of common object" show that the offence committed was immediately connected with the common object of the unlawful assembly of which the accused were members. The act must be done with a view to accomplish the common object attributed to the members of the unlawful assembly.

"Knew."-
The word "knew" indicates the state of mind at the time of the commission of the offence and not later on. Knowledge must be proved. The word "likely" means some clear evidence that the unlawful assembly had such knowledge. The prosecution must prove that the accused not only knew that the offence was likely to be committed in prosecution of the common object of the assembly.

Five or More persons —

For application of this section at least five or more persons sharing the common object is essential. The presence of five or more persons must be unquestionably proved although it may happen that some of them were unidentifiable or that their identity was doubtful. In such cases even less than five persons may be convicted.

In Kalu v. State of Madhya Pradesh -

it was held that conviction of four only under Section 149, IPC does not mean that there was no unlawful assembly. The mere fact that several accused were acquitted does not enable the four who are found guilty to contend that Section 149, IPC is inapplicable.

Distinction between common intention and common object

Distinction between common intention and common object is as follows: -

(1) The basis of liability under Section 149 is the existence of common object or Knowledge of the probability of the commission of the offence, natural consequences as the accused knew to be likely to be committed but liability under Section 34 is the existence of common intention animating the accused persons.

(2) Common intention within the meaning of Section 34 is undefined and unlimited but common object under Section 149 is defined and is limited to the five unlawful objects stated in Section 141 of the Code.

(3) Criminal act done in Section 34 must be in furtherance of common intention but criminal act under Section 149 must be done in prosecution of the common object or it would be sufficient if the members of the unlawful

assembly knew that the offence was likely to be committed.

(4) Membership of the unlawful assembly at the time of commission of crime would be sufficient for application of Section 149. Active participation in commission of crime is not necessary. But active participation in commission of crime is necessary for the application of Section 34. Some act howsoever small or insignificant must be done by every person accused of the commission of an offence.

(5) In order to hold a person liable for any offence by application of Section 149, the number of persons must be at least five or more than five because less than five persons cannot form an unlawful assembly. However, in Section 34 the offence must be committed by five or more than two persons.

(6) Section 34 defines the principle of joint liability but creates no specific offence. It has interpretative character but in Section 149 it is declaratory of the joint liability.

(7) Under Section 149, physical as well as mental state of mind at the commission of crime play a significant role on the unlawful assembly but in Section 34 physical and mental state of mind divided and placed both on the group committing the crime as well as upon the individuals constituting that group.

(8) Under Section 34, the offender is a co-sharer both in criminal act and the common intention in furtherance of which the criminal act was done. In this section, the offender is associated with the crime by both ways physically and mentally, whereas in Section 149 an individual be punished for being a member of an unlawful, assembly although he has not committed any

offence. He must be a member of an unlawful assembly at the time of commission of crime by any member of that unlawful assembly.

In Nanakchand v. State of Punjab,

it was held by the Supreme Court that the community of intention required by Section 34 is replaced in Section 149 by community of object, which is quite a different element.

In Chittarmal v. State of Rajasthan,

it was held that Section 34 as well as Section 149 deal with liability for constructive criminality, i.e., vicarious liability of a person for acts of others. Both sections deal with combination of persons who become punishable as sharers in an offence.

The "common object" is different from "common intention" However, this Court does not propose to deal into this distinction for the reason that there is no application of Section 149 and therefore this court is confined only to examine whether Section 34. IPC has rightly been applied or not and there was evidence of common intention or not. However, dealing with the said distinction in Dani Singh and others v. State of Bihar, the Court explained the term "common intention" and said that "common intention" to bring about a particular result may well develop on the spot as between a number of persons, with reference to the facts of the case and circumstances of the situation. Though common intention may develop on the spot, it must, however, be anterior in point of time to the commission of offence showing a pre-arranged plan and prior concert.

Distinction between "same or similar intention" and "common intention"-

one should not be confused with the word "same or Similar intention" with "common intention". To constitute common intention, it is necessary that intention of each one of them be known to the rest of them and shared by them. The prosecution has to lead evidence to show common intention from the act, conduct or other relevant circumstances of the case.

In Bhaba Barma and others v. State of Assam,

the Court observed that prosecution must prove facts to justify an inference that all participants of the acts had shared a common intention to commit the criminal act which was finally committed by one or more of the participants. Mere presence of a person at the time of commission of an offence by his confederates, is not, in itself sufficient to bring his case within the purview' of section 34, unless community of designs is proved against him. The Court also observed that some of the accused persons did not commit any overt act would really be of no consequence.'

Active participation of a member of the unlawful assembly.

The prosecution has been able to establish not only the appellant's presence but also his active participation as a member of the unlawful assembly. He might not have thrown the bomb at the deceased, but thereby he does not cease to be a member of the unlawful assembly as understood within the ambit of Section 149 IPC and there is ample evidence on record to safely conclude that all the accused persons who have been convicted by the High Court had formed an unlawful assembly and there was common object to assault the deceased who succumbed to the injuries inflicted on him.

Conviction of appellants.

It is a case which, falls more appropriately in situation three where the prosecution had named all those constituting the unlawful assembly. But only four of those named were eventually convicted, thereby reducing the number to less than five. There is no evidence to suggest that any one, apart from the persons named in the charge-sheet were members of the unlawful assembly, but were either not available or remained unidentified. Such being the position, the conviction of the appellant with the help of Section 149 of the IPC does not appear to be legally sustainable.

CHAPTER 4. GENERAL EXCEPTIONS (76 TO 106)

Note – Chapter given in this book are according to the chapters given in the Indian Penal Code Itself.

Introduction.

This part is very important because it deals with the various defences which a person accused of an offence can plead. General rule is that it is the duty of the prosecution to prove whether the accused had committed the crime or not. The offender has right of acquittal on the ground of benefit of doubt.

Shivaji v. State of Maharashtra,

Justice Krishna Iyer held that the benefit of doubt should always be given to the accused. He has pointed out towards the evils that too much emphasis upon this rule is likely to create. **He propounded the rule in deciding this case—**

"Benefit of doubt at the expense of social defence and to the soothing sentiment that all acquittals are always good regardless of justice to the victim and the community demand special emphasis in the contemporary context of escalating crime and escape."

K.M. Nanavati vs State of Maharashtra AIR 1962,

It was held that it is the duty of the prosecution to prove the guilt of the accused, or the accused is presumed to be innocent until his guilt is established by the prosecution beyond doubt.

General exception has two groups. -
(1) Sections 76 to 95 deal with excusable defence; and
(2) Sections 96 to 106 deal with justifiable defence.

Defence as to mistake of make of Fact. [76 and 79]

Sometimes an offence is committed by a person inadvertently. He neither intends to commit an offence nor does he know that his act is criminal. He may be totally ignorant of the existence of relevant facts. The knowledge of relevant facts is what really makes an act evil or good. Thus, if a person is not aware of the facts and acts to the best of his judgment, his act cannot be called evil. Under such circumstances he may take the plea that his acts were done under the misconception of the facts.

The provision as to defence as mistake of fact is provided under section 76 and 79 of IPC. Section 76 is related with mistake of fact as to act bound by law. Whereas section 79 is related to the mistake of fact as to act justified by law.

Section 76. Act done by a person bound, or by mistake of fact believing himself bound by law.

Nothing is an offence which is done by a person who is, or who by reason of a mistake of fact and reason of a mistake of law in good faith believes himself to be bound by law to do it.

Ingredients:
(1) Mistake of fact;
(2) Mistake of law; and
(3) In good faith believes himself to be bound by law.

Mistake of fact. –
Mistake of fact means some error of opinion as to the real facts. Mistake of fact to be excuse must be mistake in respect of a material fact or a fact essential to constitute a particular offence. It is only such ignorance that negatives the mens rea necessary to constitute the offence and as pointed out by Baron Park and by Huda. According to Huda, the guilt of the accused must depend on the circumstances as they appear to him. Mistake may be admitted as a defence.

Applicability of rule of respondent superior
The plea of obedience of an illegal order can be taken into consideration only is mitigation of punishment but cannot be pleaded as complete defence. When a constable fires upon a lawful assembly under the orders of his superior he shall be liable and cannot claim the benefit of this section because no one is obliged to obey illegal orders of the superior. Therefore, the maxim of respondent superior **has no application in this code.**

Mistake of law.
Ignorance of fact excuses and Ignorance of law does not excuse. The legal presumption that everyone knows the law even in case of a foreigner who cannot reasonably be supposed to know the law of the land have no exception. In the case of ignorance of

statute newly passed it is not necessary that it should either be published or be made known outside the country.

In good faith believes himself to be bound by law.

For claim under this section, it is necessary to show the facts which justify the belief in good faith. The private persons who are bound to assist the police under Section 42 of the Code of Criminal Procedure, 1973 will be protected under this section.

In Gopalia Kallaiya case,

A police officer came to Bombay from up country with a warrant to arrest a person and after proper enquiry on the suspicion he arrested the complainant under the warrant believing in good faith that he was the person to be arrested. In proceeding against the police officer for wrongful confinement it was held that police officers had committed no offence as he was protected by Section 76.

Section 79.

Act done by a person justified, or by mistake of fact believing himself justified by law. - Nothing is an offence which is done by any person who is justified by law, or who by reason of mistake of fact and not by reason of a mistake of law in good faith, believes himself to be justified by law in doing it.

Difference between sec 76 and 79

The only difference between sec 76 and 79 is that in section 76, a person believes that he is bound by to do a certain act while in 79, he believes that he is justified by law to do a certain act. For example, a policeman believing that a person is his senior officer and upon that person's orders fires on a mob. Here, he is bound by law to obey his senior officer's orders. But if the policeman believes that a person is a thief, he is not bound by law to arrest the person, though he is justified by law if he arrests the person. To be eligible in either of the sections, the following conditions must be satisfied -

1. It is a mistake of fact and not a mistake of law that is excusable.
2. The act must be done in good faith.

Meaning of Mistake -

A mistake means a factual error. It could be because of wrong information, i.e., ignorance or wrong conclusion. For example, an ambulance driver taking a very sick patient to a hospital may be driving faster than the speed limit in order to reach the hospital as soon as possible but upon reaching the hospital, it comes to his knowledge that the patient had died long time back and there was no need to drive fast. However, since he was ignorant of the fact, breaking the speed limit is excusable for him. A person sees someone remove a bulb from a public pole. He thinks the person is a thief and catches him and takes him to the police only to learn that the person was replacing the fused bulb. Here, he did the act in good faith but based on wrong conclusion, so his act is excusable.

To be excusable, the mistake must be of a fact and not of law. A mistake of fact means an error regarding the material facts of the situation, while a mistake of law means an error in understanding or ignorance of the law. A person who kills someone cannot take the defence of mistake saying he didn't know that killing is a crime because this is a mistake of law and not of fact. But, as in **Waryam Singh vs Emperor AIR 1926**, he can take a defence of mistake saying he believed that the killed person was a ghost because that would be a mistake of a fact.

R vs Prince, 1875 is an important case where a person was convicted of abducting a girl under 18 yrs of age. The law made taking a woman under 18 from her guardian without her guardian's permission a crime. In this case, the person had no intention to abduct her. She had gone with the person with consent and the person had no reason to believe that the girl was under 18. Further, the girl looked older than 18. However, it was held that by taking a girl without her guardian's permission, he was taking a risk and should be responsible for it because the law made it a crime even if it was done without mens rea. In this case, five rules were laid down which are guidelines whenever a question of a mistake of fact or mistake of law arises in England and elsewhere -

(1) When an act is in itself plainly criminal and is more severely punishable if certain circumstances coexist, ignorance of the existence is no answer to a charge for the aggravated offence.

(2) When an act is prima facie innocent and proper unless certain circumstances co-exist, the ignorance of such circumstances is an answer to the charge.

(3) The state of the mind of the defendants must amount to absolute ignorance of the existence of the circumstance which alters the character of the act or to a belief in its non-existence.

(4) When an act in itself is wrong, and under certain circumstances, criminal, a person who does the wrongful act cannot set up as a defence that he was ignorant of the facts which would turn the wrong into a crime.

(5) When a statute makes it penal to do an act under certain circumstances, it is a question upon the wording and object of the statute whether responsibility of

ascertaining that the circumstances exist is thrown upon the person who does the act or not. In the former case, his knowledge is immaterial.

The above guidelines were brought in Indian law in the case of **The King vs Tustipada Mandal AIR 1951 by Orissa HC.**

In **R vs Tolson 1889**, a woman's husband was believed to be dead since the ship he was traveling in had sunk. After some years, when the husband did not turn up, she married another person. However, her husband came back and since 7 years had not elapsed since his disappearance, which are required to legally presume a person dead, she was charged with bigamy. It was held that disappearance for 7 yrs is only one way to reach a belief that a person is dead. If the woman, and as the evidence showed, other people in town truly believed that the husband died in a shipwreck, this was a mistake of fact and so she was acquitted.

However, in **R vs White and R vs Stock 1921**, a person was convicted of bigamy. Here, the husband with limited literacy asked his lawyers about his divorce, who replied that they will send the papers in a couple of days. The husband construed as the divorce was done and on that belief, he married another woman. It was held that it was a mistake of law.

Good faith

Another condition that must be satisfied to take a defence of mistake of fact is that the act must be done in good faith. **Section 52** says that nothing is said to be done or believed in good faith which is done or believed without due care and attention. Thus, if one shoots an arrow in the dark without ascertaining no one is there, he cannot be excused because he failed to exercise due care.

If a person of average prudence in that situation can ascertain the facts with average diligence, a person taking the defence of mistake of those facts cannot be said to have taken due care and thus, is not excusable.

Ingredients

(1) An act done by a person under a mistake of fact;
(2) Mistake must relate to fact and not to law;
(3) Mistake must be committed in good faith; and
(4) The person doing the act is either justified by law or believes himself to be justified by law in doing an act.

Differences between Section 76 and Section 79. –

In Section 76, a person is assumed to be bound by law but in Section 79 a person is assumed to be justified by law. Under Section 76, there is a legal compulsion but under Section 79 there is a legal justification. In the case of **State of Orissa v. Bhagaban Barik,** the accused and the deceased had strained relations over grazing of cattle. On the fateful night the deceased had gone for recital of Bhagavad. Some other villagers including the accused were also present there. After the Bhagbat was over the deceased went to the pond to fetch his bell metal utensil whereupon he was given a lathi blows on his head by the accused. The defence plea was that during the day time bell metal utensil of the accused had been stolen and he was keeping a watch for the thief. He saw a person coming inside his premises and thinking him to be a thief he dealt a lathi blow but subsequently discovered that it was the deceased. It was discovered by the dying declaration made by the deceased and the extra judicial confession made by the accused that the deceased had gone to the pond after the Bhagabat to fetch his bell metal utensil. Under the circumstances, it was held that there was complete absence of good faith on the part of accused, therefore, he was not entitled to the benefit of Section 79.

Section 77. Act of Judge when acting judicially.

Nothing is an offence which is done by a Judge when acting judicially in the exercise of any power which is, or which in good faith he believes to be, given to him by law.

This section protects judges from criminal process just as Judicial Officers Protection Act, 1850, saves them from civil proceedings against them.

Section 78. Act done pursuant to the judgment or order of court.

Nothing which is done in pursuance of, or which is warranted by the judgment or order of a Court of Justice, if done whilst such judgment or order remains in force, is an offence, notwithstanding the court may have had no jurisdiction to pass such judgment or order, provided the person doing the act in good faith believes that the court had such jurisdiction.

Accident. [S. 80]

Accidents happen despite of nobody wanting them. There is no intention on the part of anybody to cause accident and so a loss caused due to an accident should not be considered a crime. This is acknowledged in Section 80 of IPC, which states thus -

Section 80. Accident in doing a lawful act. -

Nothing is an offence which is done by accident or misfortune and without any criminal intention or knowledge in doing a lawful act in a lawful manner by lawful means and with proper care and caution.

Illustration - A works with a hatchet; the head flies off and kills a person standing nearby. Here, if there was no want of proper caution on the part of A, his act is excusable and is not an offence.

From section 80, it can be seen that there are four essential conditions when a person can take the defence of an accident -

Ingredients
(1) The act must be accident or misfortune;
(2) The act must not be done with any criminal intention or knowledge;
(3) The accident must be the outcome of a lawful act done in a lawful manner by lawful means; and
(4) The act must have been done with proper care and caution.

(1) The act must be accident or misfortune;

According to **Stephen's Digest** of Criminal Law - "An event is accidental when the act by which it is caused is not done with the intention of causing it and when its occurrence as a consequence of such act is not so probable that a prudent man in the ordinary course of nature takes precautions against it. An accident does not mean a happening by but such happening must be unintentional and unexpected. In the misfortune it implies as much injury to another unconnected with the act. "Both words 'accident' and 'misfortune' deal with injury to another."

For example, a firecracker worker working with Gun powder knows that it can cause explosion and must take precaution against it. If it causes an explosion and kills a third person, he cannot claim defence of this section because the outcome was expected even though not intended.

However, if a car explodes killing a person, it is an accident because a person on average prudence does not expect a car to explode and so he cannot be expected to take precautions against it.

In the case of **State v. Ranga Swami,** it was held that shooting with an unlicensed gun does not debar an accused from claiming immunity under this section.

(2) The act must not be done with any criminal intention or knowledge;

To claim defence under this section, the act causing the accident must not be done with a bad intention or bad motive. For example, A prepares a dish for B and puts poison in it so as to kill B. However, C comes and eats the dish and dies. The death of C was indeed an accident because it was not expected by A, but the act that caused the accident was done with a criminal intention.

In **Tunda vs Rex AIR 1950**, two friends, who were fond of wrestling, were wresting and one got thrown away on a stone and died. This was held to be an accident and since it was not done without any criminal intention, the defendant was acquitted.

(3) The accident must be the outcome of a lawful act done in a lawful manner by lawful means.

An accident that happens while doing an unlawful act is no defence. Not only that, but the act must also be done in a lawful manner and by lawful means. For example, requesting rent payment from a renter is a lawful act but threatening him with a gun to pay rent is not lawful manner and if there is an accident due to the gun and if the renter gets hurt or killed, defence under this section cannot be claimed.

In **Jogeshshwar vs Emperor**, where the accused was fighting with a man and the man's pregnant wife intervened. The accused aimed at the woman but accidently hit the baby who was killed. He was not allowed protection under this section because he was not doing a lawful act in a lawful manner by lawful means.

In the case of **Shakir Khan v. Crown,** a big party consisting of some hundred men went out for shooting pigs. A boar rushed towards the accused who fired at her, but he missed the boar and the shot struck the leg of a member of the party. It was held that the death was caused by accident and was not the result of rash and negligent shooting.

(4) The act must have been done with proper care and caution.

The act that causes the harm must have been done with proper care and precautions. An accident caused due to negligence is not excusable. A person must take precautions for any effects that any person with average intelligence would anticipate. For example, an owner of a borewell must fence the hole to prevent children falling into it because any person with average prudence can anticipate that a child could fall into an open borewell.

In **Bhupendra Singh Chudasama vs State of Gujarat 1998**, the appellant, an armed constable of SRPF shot at his immediate supervisor while the latter was inspecting the dam site in dusk hours. The appellant took the plea that it was dark at that time, and he saw someone moving near the dam with fire. He thought that there was a miscreant. He shouted to stop the person but upon getting no response he fired the shot. However, it was proven that the shot was fired from a close range, and it was held that he did not take enough precaution before firing the shot and was convicted.

Other cases.

State of Orissa v. Khora Ghasi,

In another case of **State of Orissa v. Khora Ghasi,** the accused caused the death of the deceased by shooting arrow under the bona fide belief that he was shooting that arrow at a bear which had entered into his field and was destroying his maize crop. It was held that death caused by him was accidental.

Raja Ram v. State.

In Raja Ram v. State, accused fired his gun on his assailant to defend his person but assailant escaped his injury and shot the other four persons one of whom died. In the absence of evidence that the accused intended to cause the injury to the injured persons it was held that he was entitled to protection under Sections 80, 96 and 100 of the Indian Penal Code.

Sukhdev Singh v. N.C.T. Delhi

it was held by the Supreme Court that Section 80 of Indian Penal Code exempts the doer of an innocent or lawful act in an innocent and lawful manner from any unforeseen result that may ensue from accident or misfortune if either of these elements is wanting the act will not be excused on the ground of accident.

Accident in an act done with consent

Section 87 extends the scope of accident to cases where an act was done with the consent of the victim. It says thus -

Section 87 - Nothing which is not intended to cause death or grievous hurt and which is not known to the doer to be likely to cause death or grievous hurt is an offence by reason of any harm that it may cause or be intended by the doer to cause to any person above eighteen years of age, who has given consent whether express or implied, to suffer that harm; or by reason of any harm which it may be known by the doer to be likely to cause to any such person who has consented to take the risk of that harm.

Illustration - A and Z agree to fence with each other for amusement. This agreement implies the consent by each to suffer any harm which in the course of such fencing may be caused without foul play; and if A, while playing fairly, hurts Z, A commits no offence.

This is based on the premise that everybody is the best judge for himself. If a person knowingly undertakes a task that is likely to cause certain damage, then he cannot hold anybody responsible for suffering that damage. Thus, a person watching another lighting up firecrackers agrees to take the risk of getting burned and must not hold anybody responsible if he gets burned.

In Nageswara vs Emperor, a person asked the accused to try Dao on his hand believing that his hand was Dao proof due to a charm. He got hurt and bled to death. However, the accused was acquitted because he was protected under this section. The deceased consented to the risk of trying Dao on his hand.

Necessity [S. 81]

Section 81. Act likely to cause harm but done without criminal intent and to prevent other harm. -

Nothing is an offence merely by reason of its being done with the knowledge that it is likely to cause harm if it be done without any criminal intention to cause harm, and in good faith for the purpose of preventing or avoiding other harm to person or property.

Explanation. - it is a question of fact in such a case whether the harm to be prevented or avoided was of such a nature and so imminent as to justify or excuse the risk of doing the act with the knowledge that it was likely to cause harm.

Ingredients

(1) The act constituting the offence is known by the wrongdoer to be likely to cause harm, but it is done without any criminal intention to cause harm;

(2) The act must have been done in good faith;

(3) The act must also have been done for the purpose of preventing or avoiding other harm; and

(4) The harm aimed to be prevented or avoided may relate to person or property.

Example. -

A in a great fire, pulls down many houses of another person in order to prevent the fire from spreading he does it without the intention to damage the house of those persons in good faith of saving human life or property. There, if it be found that harm to be prevented was of such a nature and so imminent to excuse 'A's act. A is not guilty of the offence.

Act of child, insanity, intoxication (82 to 84)

As mentioned before, to hold a person legally responsible for a crime, in general, evil intention must be proved. A person who is not mentally capable of distinguishing between good and bad or of understanding the implications of an action cannot be said to have an evil intention and thus should not be punished.

Such incapacity may arise due to age, mental illness, or intoxication. Let us look at each of these one by one.

Act of a child

It is assumed that a child does not have an evil mind and he does not do things with evil intention. He cannot even fully understand the implications of the act that he is doing. Thus, he completely lacks mens rea and should not be punished. IPC contains for following exemptions for a child -

Section 82. Act of child under seven years of age. –

Nothing is an offence which is done by a child under seven years of age.

Section 83. Act of a child above seven years and under twelve of immature understanding. –

Nothing is an offence which is done by a child above seven years of age and under twelve, who has not attained sufficient maturity of understanding to judge of the nature and consequences of his conduct on that occasion.

Through these sections, IPC acknowledges the fact that children under seven years of age cannot have sufficient maturity to commit a crime and is completely excused. In Indian law, a child below seven years of age is called **Doli Incapax**.

In **Queen vs Lukhini Agradanini 1874**, it was held that merely the proof of age of the child would be a conclusive proof of innocence and would ipso facto be an answer to the charge against him.

However, a child above seven but below twelve may or may not have sufficient maturity to commit a crime and whether he is sufficiently mature to understand the nature and consequences of the act needs to be determined from the facts of the case.

Ingredients of section 83

(1) An act done by a child above seven years of age but under the age of twelve years;
(2) The child must not have sufficient maturity of understanding to judge of the nature and consequence of his conduct; and
(3) Incapacity must exist at the time of the commission of the act.

Section 83 provides qualified immunity because presumes that a child above seven and below twelve has sufficient maturity to commit a crime and the burden is on the defence to prove that he did not possess sufficient maturity to commit crime.

Thus, in **Hiralal vs State of Bihar 1977**, the boy who participated in a concerted action and used a sharp weapon for a murderous attack, was held guilty in the absence of any evidence leading to boy's feeble understanding of his actions.

In **English law,** a boy below 14 years is deemed incapable of raping a woman, but no such protection is offered in India.

In **Emperor vs Paras Ram Dubey**, a boy of 12 years of age was convicted of raping a girl.

Thus section 82 and 83 are as follows-

Section 83 deals with qualified immunity a child under the age of twelve years but above the age of 7 years possessed maturity of understanding and has the capacity to commit the crime. Criminal liability under this section is rebuttable only on the proof the defendant by the conduct of the child. A child coming within the view of Section 83 is qualified to avail the defence of doli incapax if it is proved that he has not attained sufficient maturity of understanding the nature and consequences of his conduct.

The test of qualified immunity -
(1) The nature of the act done;
(2) Subsequent conduct of the offender; and
(3) Demeanour and appearance of the offender in the court.

Distinction between Indian Law and English law. -

In India, a child above seven years of age but under the age of twelve years enjoys a qualified immunity and is presumed to be doli incapax whereas in English law this is available to a child over 10 years but under the age of 14 years.

The absence of evidence leading about the boys feeble understanding of his actions the defence was not allowed. - In the case of **Hiralal v. State of Bihar**, the boy participated in a concerted action and used a sharp weapon for a murderous attack on the deceased. In the absence of evidence leading about the boys feeble understanding of his actions the defence under Section 83 was not allowed.

Act done to effectuate the intention; Defence is not allowed. –

In the **case of Ulla Mohapatra**, the accused, a boy of over 11 years but below 12 years picked up a knife and threatened to cut the deceased to pieces and did actually kill him. It was held that his action could lead to only one inference, namely, that he did what he intended to do, and that he knew, all along, that one blow inflicted with a knife would effectuate his intention. He was sent to Reformatory school for 5 years.

Defence of Insanity [84]

A person may be rendered incapable of judging an action as right or wrong due to several kinds of deficiency in mental faculty or a disease of mind. Such people are called insane. Their position is same as children below the age of discretion. From time to time several approaches have been adopted to understand insanity and to see whether a person was insane or not at the time of his act.

Section 84. Act of a person of unsound mind.

Nothing is an offence which is done by a person who, at the time of doing it, by reason of unsoundness of mind, is incapable of knowing the nature of the act, or that he is doing what is either wrong or contrary to law.

Ingredients. -

Under Section 84, ingredients are as follows: -
(1) Act must be done by a person of unsound mind;
(2) Such person must be incapable of knowing the nature of the act, that the act was contrary to law or that the act was wrong;
(3) Such insanity must be by reason of unsoundness of mind of the offender; and
(4) **Such incapacity must exist at the time of the act** -

Thus, a person claiming immunity under this section must prove the existence of the following conditions -

(1) Act must be done by a person of unsound mind;

Unsound Mind is not defined in IPC. As per Stephen, it is equivalent to insanity, which is a state of mind where the functions of feeling, knowing, emotion, and willing are performed in abnormal manner. The term Unsoundness of mind is quite wide and includes all varieties of want of capacity whether temporary or permanent, or because of illness or birth defect. However, mere unsoundness of mind is not a sufficient ground. It must be accompanied with the rest of the conditions.

(2) Such incapacity must exist at the time of the act -

A person may become temporarily out of mind or insane for example due to epilepsy or some other disease. However, such condition must exist at the time of the act.

In **S K Nair vs State of Punjab 1997**, the accused was charged for murder of one and grievous assault on other two. He pleaded insanity. However, it was held that the words spoken by the accused at the time of the act clearly show that he understood what he was doing and that it was wrong. Thus, he was held guilty.

(3) Such person must be incapable of knowing the nature of the act, that the act was contrary to law or that the act was wrong;

Due to incapacity, he was incapable of knowing -

1. The nature of the act. or
2. That the act is wrong. or
3. That the act is contrary to law.

The accused in not protected if he knows that what he was doing was wrong even if he did not know that what he was doing was contrary to law.

Chhagan vs State 1976,

It was held that mere queerness on the part of the accused or the crime does not establish that he was insane. It must be proved that the cognitive faculties of the person are such that he does not know what he has done or what will follow his act.

In general, to hold a person legally responsible for a crime intention is necessary and after that capacity to commit a crime in a position to judge its right or wrong. Onus of proving the unsoundness of mind is on the accused.

Shrikant AnandRao Bhosale v. State of Maharashtra,

It was held that keeping in view the totality of facts and circumstances in the light of the evidence on record the accused was suffering from paranoid schizophrenia. The unsoundness of mind before and after the incident would be a relevant fact. From the circumstances of the case an inference can reasonably be drawn that the accused was under a delusion at the relevant time.

Wild Beast Test

This test was evolved in **R vs Arnold 1724**. Here, the accused was tried for wounding and attempting to kill Lord On slow. By evidence, it was clear that the person was mentally deranged. J Tracy laid the test as follows, "If he was under the visitation of God and could not distinguish between good and evil and did not know what he did, though he committed the greatest offence, yet he could not be guilty of any offence against any law whatsoever."

Insane Delusion Test

This test was evolved in **Hadfield's Case in 1800**, where Hadfield was charged with high treason and attempting the assassination of King George III. He was acquitted on the ground of insane delusion. Here, the counsel pleaded that insanity was to be determined by the fact of fixed insane delusions with which the accused was suffering, and which were the direct cause of his crime. He pointed out that there are people who are deprived of their understanding, either permanently or temporarily, and suffer under delusions of alarming description which overpowers the faculties of their victims.

McNaughton's Rules

McNaughton Rule is the basis of the modern law on the insanity which was propounded by fifteen Judge Bench of House of Lords. Facts of this case is that a Scotsman was tried for the murder of Edmond Drummond, Private Secretary of Sir Robert Peel, the then Prime Minister. Denial McNaughton was under an insane delusion that, Sir Robert Peel has injured him and mistaking Drummond for Sir Robert Peel he shot and killed him. The accused pleaded insanity in his defence and produced medical evidence which showed that he was labouring under a morbid delusion because of which he lost his power of control. The accused was acquitted on the ground of insanity. His acquittal became the debate in the House of Lords and then fifteen Judges bench was constituted to solve the problem. Law relating to insanity was first came into existence in the modern society. The very first it was said that due to lack of knowing the nature and consequence of act an insane person is discharged from his liability arising out of any criminal act.

1. Regardless of the fact that the accused was under insane delusion, he is punishable according to the nature of the crime if, at the time of the act, he knew that he was acting contrary to law.
2. Every man must be presumed to be sane until contrary is proven. That is, to establish defence on the ground of insanity, it must be clearly proven that the person suffered from a condition due to which he was not able to understand the nature of the act or did not know what he was doing was wrong.
3. If the accused was conscious that the act was one that he ought not to do and if that act was contrary to law, he was punishable.

4. If the accused suffers with partial delusion, he must be considered in the same situation as to the responsibility, as if the facts with respect to which the delusion exists were real. **For example,** if the accused, under delusion that a person is about to kill him and attacks and kills the person in self-defence, he will be exempted from punishment. But if the accused, under delusion that a person has attacked his reputation, and kills the person due to revenge, he will be punishable.
5. A medical witness who has not seen the accused previous to the trial should not be asked his opinion whether on evidence he thinks that the accused was insane.

The Indian Law recognizes the first two principals and incorporates them in section 84.

KINDS OF UNSOUNDNESS OF MIND

1. Idiot. –

A person who is of non-sane memory by birth a perpetual infirmity, without lucid intervals is said to be an idiot. Idiot is also the person who is unable to know who his father or mother, unable to count numbers as 1, 2, 3 or fifty or tell the name of the days of the week.

2. Lunatic. –

A person suffering from periodic mental disorder is known as lunatic. Madness is permanent.

3. Non compo mentis. -

A person non compo mentis by illness is exempted from criminal liability, in cases of such acts which are committed while under the influence of his mental disorder.

4. Disease of mind. –

The accused must first of all have to prove that he was suffering from a disease of the mind when he did the prohibited act.

In the case of **Sudhir Chand Biswas v. State**, it was held that in the case of murder insanity is a recognised exception to the criminal liability under Section 84.

Ramlal v. State of Rajasthan. - Fact of this case is that Ramlal was accused of killing a boy 8yearold. According to the doctor, he was patient of epilepsy with retarted mental faculty so as to put him in the category of severe sub normality. Running away to his village after the commission of crime shows that he was conscious of the act what he had done and it was enough to defeat the plea of insanity.

Shri Ram v. State of Maharashtra. - In this case, the accused killed his three infant granddaughters with a handle of grinding stone. The accused did not try to conceal himself from the public and there was no evidence to destroy the evidence of crime. It was held that in absence of mens rea on the part of the accused he was liable to be discharged of his criminal liability under Section 84 of the Indian Penal Code.

Applicability of section. –

Hari Singli God v. State of M.P.,

In this case, it was held that the standard to be applied for deciding the applicability of Section 84 of IPC is whether according to the ordinary standard, adopted by a reasonable man, the act was right or wrong. The mere fact that an accused is conceited odd irascible and his brain is not quite all right or that the physical and mental ailments from which he suffered had rendered his intellect weak in and had affected his emotions and will, or that he had committed certain unusual acts, in the past or that he was liable to recurring fits of insanity at short intervals, or that he was subject to getting epileptic fits but there was nothing abnormal in his behaviour, or that his behaviour was queer cannot be sufficient to attract the application of Section 84. It was held on facts of case that Section 84 had no application.

Claim of benefit. –

State of Rajasthan v. Vidhya Devi.

In this case, accused was admitted to hospital even before challan was filed. He remained under treatment for 9 months. It was held that the accused was entitled to claim the benefit of Section 84, IPC as circumstances clearly show insanity of accused.

Legality of conviction. –

Sudhakaran v. State of Kerala,

In this case, the accused vas alleged to have committed murder of his wife. While he had brutally committed murder of his wife, he did not cause any hurt or discomfort to his child. Rather he made up his mind to ensure that child be put into proper care and custody after murder. In his defence, he pleaded unsoundness of mind. He was suffering from paranoid schizophrenia. It was held that the burden is on the accused to prove that by reason of unsoundness of mind, he was incapable of showing the nature of the act committed by him. The crucial point of time at which the unsoundness of mind should be established is the time when offence is committed- In this case, conduct of accused before and after incident was held sufficient to negate any notion that he was mentally insane so as not to be possessed of necessary mens rea for committing murder of his wife. Only evidence placed on record shows that the accused had been treated in psychiatric Hospital for 13 days some 15 years prior to the incident and Doctor had diagnosed deceased as psychotic disorder. Therefore, his conviction for murder was held to be proper.

Intoxication. [85 and 86]

Several times intoxication due to drinking alcohol or taking other substances cause the person to lose the judgment of right or wrong. In early law, however, this was no defence for criminal responsibility. In recent times this has become a valid defence but only if the intoxication was involuntary.

The Provision related to defence of intoxication is given under section 85 and 86. Section 85 provides for the intoxication against will or involuntary intoxication. Whereas the section 86 provides for the involuntary intoxication.

Section 85. Act of a person incapable of judgment by reason of intoxication against his will. –

Nothing is an offence which is done by a person who, at the time of doing it, is by reason of intoxication, incapable of knowing the nature of the act, or that he is doing what is either wrong or contrary to law; provided that the thing which intoxicated him was given to him against his will or without his knowledge.

Ingredients.

(1) At the time of doing the act by reason of intoxication he was incapable of knowing;

(2) The nature of the act or that he was doing what was either wrong or contrary to law; and

(3) That the thing which intoxicated him was administered to him without his knowledge or against his will.

Voluntary drunkenness is no excuse for the commission of crime.

Involuntary drunkenness is excused when a person is unable to distinguish whether the act is right or wrong. For protection under this section drunkenness must be against his will.

Director of Public Prosecution vs Beard,

In this case, a girl of thirteen years while going to market passed through the gate of a mill where the accused Beard was a watchman and at that time he was on duty. The accused attempted to commit rape to the girl. The girl struggled; therefore, the accused placed his hand over her mouth and pressed his thumb on her throat in a bid to prevent her from screaming. The girl was killed unintentionally. The Court of Appeal found him guilty of the manslaughter, but the House of Lords restored him for conviction of murder. His conduct shows that he was in a conscious state therefore a plea for Section 85 was rejected.

The following principles were laid down in this case -

1. If the accused was so drunk that he was incapable of forming the intent required, he could not be convicted of a crime for which only intent was required to be proved.

2. Insanity whether produced by drunkenness or otherwise is a defence to the crime charged. The difference between being drunk and diseases to which drunkenness leads is another. The former is no excuse, but the latter is a valid defence if it causes insanity.

3. The evidence of drunkenness falling short of proving incapacity in the accused to form the intent necessary to commit a crime and merely establishing that his mind was affected by the drink so that he more readily gave way to violent passion does not rebut the presumption that a man intends the natural consequences of the act.

Section 86. Offence requiring a particular intent or knowledge committed by one who is intoxicated. –
In cases, where an act done is not an offence unless done with a particular knowledge or intent, a person who does the act in a state of intoxication shall be liable to be dealt with as if he had the same knowledge as he would have had if he had not been intoxicated, unless the thing which intoxicated him was administered to him without his knowledge or against his will.

A person intoxicated voluntarily will be treated as he has the same knowledge if he had not been intoxicated. He habitual drunkenness causes any mental disease and affects the mind such disease is looked upon as insanity.

R v. Lipman,

In this case Lipman and the deceased girl were both drug addict. On one evening Lipman consumed a quantity of L.S.D. (drug) at her flat. He began to suffer an illusion of descending to the centre of the earth and being attacked by snakes with which he fought. in feeling this, he struck her blows on the head causing her to die from asphyxia. Lipman was convicted for manslaughter. It was observed that for the purposes of criminal responsibility no distinction is made between the effects of drugs voluntarily taken and involuntarily taken no specific intent is necessary to support a conviction for manslaughter based on a killing in the course of unlawful act and when a killing results from an unlawful act no specific intent has to be proved to convict of manslaughter and thus self-induced intoxication is no defence.

Basudev v. State of Pepsu,

In this case, the Supreme Court held that so far as knowledge is concerned, we must attribute to the intoxicated man the same knowledge as if he was quite sober. But so far as the intention is concerned we must gather it from the attending general circumstances of the case paying due regard to the degree of intoxication if a man had not gone such a deep drinking that he is unable to judge what he has done is good or bad.

A.G. for Northern Ireland v. Gallagher,

This case is popularly known as Gallagher's case, the accused was a psychopath and due to this he was suffering from a disease of mind which would be aggravated by drink in such a way as to cause him the more readily to lose his self-control. The accused Gallagher indicated his intention to kill his wife then went to market and purchased bottle of whiskey and drunk of it before he in fact killed his wife with a knife. In this case, it was held that a psychopath who goes out intending to kill knowing it is wrong and does kill cannot escape the consequences by making himself drunk before doing it.

While specific intent has to be proved to convict of manslaughter and thus self-induced intoxication is no defence.

Consent (87 to 92)

Section 87. Act not intended and not known to be likely to cause death or grievous hurt, done by consent. –

Nothing which is not intended to cause death or grievous hurt and which is not known by the doer to be likely to cause death or grievous hurt, is an offence by reason of any harm which it may cause or be intended by the doer to cause, to any person above eighteen years of age, who has given consent, whether express or implied to suffer that harm, or by reason of any harm which it may be known by the doer to be likely to cause any such person who has consented to take the risk to that harm.

Ingredients

(1) If the act is done neither with the intention of causing death or grievous hurt nor the knowledge that it is likely to cause death or grievous hurt;
(2) Harm is caused to any person with his consent;
(3) Person giving consent is above eighteen years of age; and
(4) Consent given may be expressed or implied.

Deceased's consent is no defence in the absence of good reason. There is no definition of consent in the Indian Penal Code. Where an act is unlawful itself the defence of consent cannot be pleaded. This section is based on the Roman maxim **volenti non fit injuria** which means that a person who voluntarily takes risk. Generally, games like boxing, fencing, etc. are the games in which participant has risk of injuries, without any criminal intention or knowledge. Probably death may be a result of that game. According to this section participants take risk of injury or assault and during the game if anyone gets injury, another can plead the protection of Section 87.

For Example. -'A' and 'B' agree to fence with each other for amusement. The agreement implies the consent of each to suffer any harm which, in the course of such fencing may be caused without any criminal intent and without foul play and if 'A', while playing fairly hurts 'B', 'A' has committed no offence.

Section 88. Act not intended to cause death, done by consent in good faith for person's benefit. - –

Nothing which is not intended to cause death, is an offence by reason of any harm which it may cause, or be intended by the doer to cause, or be known by the doer to be likely to cause, to any person for whose benefit it is done in good faith, and who has given a consent whether express or implied to suffer that harm, or to take -the risk of that harm

Ingredients -

(1) The act done is for the benefit of the person who suffers injury;

(2) Such act is done with the consent of the person to suffer that take the risk of that harm;

(3) Consent may be express or implied;

(4) Act is done in good faith; and

(5) Act is done without intention to cause death though it might have been done with the intention of causing such harm as may result in death.

Act is done for the benefit of the person. - Plea for defence under this section is available when it is necessary to do that act for the benefit of that person, mere **pecuniary benefit does not fall** within the meaning of this section or Sections 89 and 92.

Act is done with the consent. - Act must be done with the consent of the sufferer.

Consent must be express or implied. - Consent must be given by such person who is capable by law to give it.

Act must be done in good faith. - Act which results in the harm must be done in good faith to cause harm but not death.

Section 89. Act done in good faith for the benefit of child or insane person by consent of guardian. –

Nothing which is done in good faith for the benefit of a person under twelve years of age, or of unsound mind, or by consent, either express or implied, of a guardian or other person having lawful charge to that person, is an offence by reason of any harm which it may cause, or be intended by the doer to cause or be known by the doer to be likely to cause to that person.

Provisos.

First. - That this exception shall not extend to the intentional causing death, or attempting to cause death;

Secondly. -That this exception shall not extend to the doing of anything which the person doing it knows to be likely to cause death for any purpose other than the preventing of death or grievous disease or infirmity;

Thirdly. -That the exception shall not extend to the voluntary causing of grievous hurt, or to the attempting to cause grievous hurt, unless it be for the purpose of preventing death or grievous hurt or the curing of any grievous disease or infirmity;

Fourthly. – That this exception shall not extend to the abetment of any offence to the committing of which offence it would not extend.

Ingredients

(1) Act must be done for the benefit of a person who is either a minor under twelve years of age or a person of unsound mind;

(2) Act must be done **in good faith**;

(3) Act must be done by the guardian or by the consent of the guardian or other person having lawful charge of that person; and

(4) Consent may either be **express or implied**.

Illustration. –

A, in good faith, for his child's benefit without his child's consent has his child cut by a surgeon for the purpose of operation knowing that it will cause the child's death not intending to cause the child's death, objecting to cure the child A is within the exception.

Section 90. Consent known to be given under fear or misconception.

A consent is not such a consent as is intended by any section of this Code if the consent is given by a person under fear of injury or under misconception of fact and if the person doing the act knows or has reason to believe that the consent was given in consequence of such fear or misconception; or

Consent of insane person – If the consent is given by a person who from unsoundness of mind or intoxication is unable to understand the nature and consequence of that to which he gives his consent; or

Consent of child. - Unless the contrary appears from the context if the consent is given by a person who is under **twelve years of age**.

Ingredients

(1) Consent given by a person under fear of injury,
(2) Consent given under misconception of fact;
(3) Consent given by a child under 12 years of age;
(4) Consent given by a person of unsound mind; and
(5) Consent given by an intoxicated person.

Case of Dasrath Paswan

the accused has failed at an examination at three successive years. He was very much upset at these failures accordingly he decided to end his life. He informed of his decision to his wife who was a literate woman of 19 years of age. His wife asked him to kill her first and then kill himself. In consequence of this pact, the accused killed her but arrested before he could kill himself. It was held that the wife does not consent her husband under fear of injury or misconception. The accused would not be liable for murder but for culpable homicide not amounting to murder.

Udaya v. State of Karnataka,

It was held by Supreme Court that consent given by prosecutrix to sexual intercourse cannot be said to be given under misconception of fact; i.e., promise to marry because she also desired for it. Further a false promise to marry is not a fact within the meaning of the penal code.

Section 91. Exclusion of acts which are offences independently of harm caused. –

The exception of Sections 87, 88, 89 do not extend to acts which are offences independently of any harm which they may cause, or be intended to cause or be known to be likely to cause to the person giving the consent or on whose behalf the consent is given.

Example. –

Causing miscarriage (unless caused in good faith for the purpose of saving the life of the woman) is an offence independently of any harm which it may cause or be intended to cause to the woman. Therefore, it is not an offence by reason of such harm and consent of the woman or of her guardian to the causing of such miscarriage does not justify the act-

Section 92. Act done in good faith for the benefit of a person without consent. –

Nothing is an offence by reason of any harm which it may cause to a person for whose benefit it is done in good faith, even without that person's consent, if the circumstances are such that it is impossible for that person to signify consent, or if that person is incapable of giving consent and has no guardian or other person in lawful charge of him from whom it is possible to obtain consent in time for things to be done with benefit.

Provisos:

First. - That this exception shall not extend to the intentional causing death or attempting to cause death.

Second. - That this exception shall not extend to the doing of anything which the person doing it knows to be likely to cause death for any purpose other than the preventing of death or grievous hurt or the curing of any grievous disease or infirmity.

Third. -That this exception shall not extend to the voluntary causing of hurt or to attempting to cause hurt for any purpose other than the preventing of death or hurt.

Fourth - That this exception shall not extend to the abetment of any offence to the committing of which offence it would not extend.

Explanation, - Mere pecuniary benefit is not benefit within the meaning of sections 88, 89 and 92.

Ingredients

(1) Act must be done for the benefit of the person;
(2) Act must be done in good faith;
(3) Act must be reasonable in the circumstances of the case;
(4) Act may be done without that person's consent or without the consent of some person on his behalf; and
(5) Act must be done without any criminal intention or knowledge.

Example. - B is carried off by a tiger. A fire at the tiger knowing it to be likely that the shot may kill B but not intending to kill B and in good faith intending B's benefit. A's bullet gives B a mortal wound. A has committed no offence.

Other Defences and Provisions. [93 to 95]

Section 93. Communication made in good faith. –

No communication made in good faith is an offence by reason of any harm to the person to whom it is made, if it is made for the benefit of that person.

Ingredients
(1) Communication made in good faith; and
(2) For the **benefit of the person** to whom it is made.

This section is made for the protection of doctors. Very often it becomes necessary to warn the patient that his end was near so that he might make his will or arrange his affairs to his own satisfaction. Doctor will be protected under this section if a patient dies due to reaction of communication made to him. The word 'harm" in this section means an injurious mental reaction.

Example. -A, a surgeon, in good faith, communicates to a patient his opinion that he cannot live. The patient dies in consequence of the shock. A has committed no offence, though he knew it to be likely that the communication might cause the patient's death.

Section 94. Act to which a person is compelled by threats. –

Except murder, and offences against the State punishable with death, nothing is an offence which is done by a person who is compelled to do it by threats, which, at the time of doing it, reasonably cause the apprehension that instant death to that person will otherwise be the consequence:

Provided that the person doing the act did not, of his own accord or from a reasonable apprehension of harm to himself short of instant death, place himself in a situation by which he became subject to such constraint.

Explanation 1. -A person, who of his own accord, or by reason of a threat of being beaten, joins a gang of dacoits knowing their character, is not entitled to the benefit of this exception on the ground of his having been compelled by his associates to do anything that is an offence by law.

Explanation 2. -A person seized by a gang of dacoits, and forced, by threat of instant death, to do a thing which is an offence by law; for example, a smith compelled to take his tools and to force the door of a house for the dacoits to enter and plunder it, is entitled to the benefit of this exception.

Ingredients

1. That the person **did not voluntarily** expose himself to the constraint;
2. That the fear which prompted his action was the fear of instant death; and
3. That the act itself was done at a time when he was left with no option but to do it or die.

This exception is based on the principle that an act done by me against my will is not my act. Voluntary act is necessary to constitute a crime.

In the case of Magan Lal, it was held that except murder and offences punishable with death compulsion is an excusable defence if the act is done under the fear of instant death therefore if murder is committed under a threat of instant death is not excused, abetment of murder will be excused under this section.

Section 95. Act causing slight harm. – [De minimis non Curat lex]

Nothing is an offence by reason that it causes, or that it is intended to cause, or that it is known to be likely to cause any harm, if that harm is so slight that no person of ordinary sense and temper would complain of such harm.

This section is based on the principle contained in the maxim **de minimis non curat lex** which means that the law takes no account of trifles. No prudent man complains of mere trifles. The word 'harm' is used in this section in a very wide sense and it includes physical injury also.

In the case of **Public Prosecutor v. K. Satyanarayan**, it was held that conduct of lawyers in using filthy language in the course of cross-examination comes under the protection of this section.

In another case of Anoop Krishna Sharma v. State, it was held by the Bombay High Court that where the accused locked the complainant inside the factory by pulling down the shutter, it was held that offence under Section 342 of the Indian Penal Code for wrongful confinement were established but as the complainant regained his freedom within a very short time and only a minimum harm was caused or the harm which was caused was very slight the case will be clearly coverable by Section 95.

Section 95 and Adulteration Act. –

It was discussed in the case of State of Maharashtra v. Taher Bhai, wherein the two accused persons were found selling hard boiled sugar confectionery in contravention of the rules framed in Food Adulteration Act. It was held that Section 95 is not applicable to any offence under the Prevention of Food Adulteration Act. A slight deviation from the standard fixed under the rule is not going to cause slight harm as contemplated under Section 95 of the Indian Penal Code.

THE RIGHT OF PRIVATE DEFENCE (96 to 106)

It is said that the law of self-defence is not written but is born with us. We do not learn it or acquire it somehow, but it is in our nature to defend and protect ourselves from any kind of harm. When one is attacked by robbers, one cannot wait for law to protect oneself. Bentham has said that fear of law can never restrain bad men as much as the fear of individual resistance and if you take away this right then you become accomplice of all bad men.

IPC incorporates this principle in section 96, which says,

Section 96. Things done in private defence. –

Nothing is an offence which is done m the exercise of the right of private defence.

There is no right of private defence under the Code against any act which is not itself an offence under it. There are certain limitations on the right of private defence of person or property.

1. There must be a reasonable apprehension of death or grievous hurt which amounts to causing death or damage to the property concerned;
2. More harm than that is necessary to save the person or property should not be caused; and
3. That if there is sufficient time for recourse to public authorities, the right is not available.

No private defence is available in the case of free fight.

STATE OF U.P. V. PUSSLE,

In this case, it was held that a person who is an aggressor and who seeks attack on himself by his own aggressive attack cannot rely upon the right of private defence.

HAKIM SINGH V. STATE OF M.P.,

In this case the deceased was unarmed when fired at, he caused injury only after receiving a gunshot wound, right of private defence in shooting at him not available.

SHAJAHAN AND OTHERS V. STATE OF KERALA,

In this case, it was held by the Supreme Court that the burden of proving self-defence lies on accused. It was further observed that the right of private defence is essentially a defensive right circumscribed by the governing statute, i.e., Indian Penal Code. It is available only when circumstances clearly justify it. It cannot be pleaded or availed as a pretext for a vindictive, aggressive or retributive purpose of offence.

In Section 97 through 106, IPC defines the characteristics and scope of private defence in various situations.

Section 97. Right of private defence of the body and of property. –

Every person has a right, subject to the restriction contained in Section 99, to defend -

First. -His own body, and the body of any other person, against any offence affecting the human body;

Secondly. -The property, whether movable or immovable, of himself or of any other person, against any act which is an offence falling under the definition of theft, robbery, mischief or criminal trespass.

This allows a person to defend his or anybody else's body or property from being unlawfully harmed. Under English law, the right to defend the person and property against unlawful aggression was limited to the person himself or kindred relations or to those having community of interest e.g., parent and child, husband and wife, landlord and tenant, etc. However, this section allows this right to defend an unrelated person's body or property as well. Thus, it is apt to call it as right to private defence instead of right to self-defence.

It is important to note that the right exists only against an act that is an offence. There is no right to defend against something that is not an offence. For example, a policeman has the right to handcuff a person on his belief that the person is a thief and so his act of handcuffing is not an offence and thus the person does not have any right under this section.

Similarly, an aggressor does not have this right. An aggressor himself is doing an offence and even if the person being aggressed upon gets the better of the aggressor in the exercise of his right to self-defence, the aggressor cannot claim the right of self-defence. As held by SC in **Mannu vs State of UP AIR 1979**, when the deceased was waylaid and attacked by the accused with dangerous weapons the question of self-defence by the accused did not arise.

The right to private defence of the body exists against any offence towards human body, the right to private defence of the property exists only against an act that is either theft, robbery, mischief, or criminal trespass or is an attempt to do the same.

Ram Rattan vs State of UP 1977, SC

In this case, it was observed that a true owner has every right to dispossess or throw out a trespasser while the trespasses is in the act or process of trespassing and has not accomplished his possession, but this right is not available to the true owner if the trespasser has been successful in accomplishing the possession to the knowledge of the true owner. In such circumstances the law requires that the true owner should dispossess the trespasser by taking resource to the remedies available under the law.

Restrictions on right to private defence

As with any right, the right to private defence is not an absolute right and is neither unlimited. It is limited by the following restrictions imposed by section 99 -

Section 99 - Restrictions

There is no right of private defence against an act which does not reasonably cause the apprehension of death or of grievous hurt, if done, or attempted to be done, by a public servant acting in good faith under colour of his office though that act may not be strictly justifiable by law.

There is no right of private defence against an act which does not reasonably cause the apprehension of death or of grievous hurt, if done, or attempted to be done, by the direction of a public servant acting in good faith under colour of his office though that direction may not be strictly justifiable by law.

There is no right of private defence in cases in which there is time to have recourse to the protection of the public authorities.

Extent to which the right may be exercised - The right of private defence in no case extends to the inflicting of more harm that it is necessary to inflict for the purpose of defence.

Explanation 1 - A person is not deprived of his right of private defence against an act done or attempted to be done by a public servant, as such, unless he knows or has reason to believe that the person doing the act is such public servant.

Explanation 2 - A person is not deprived of his right of private defence against an act done or attempted to be done by the direction of a public servant, unless he knows or has reason to believe that the person doing the act is acting by such direction, or unless such person states the authority under which he acts or if he has authority in writing, unless he produces such authority if demanded.

Upon carefully examining this section, we can see that the right to private defence is not available in the following conditions -

1. when an act is done by a public servant or upon his direction and the act

   1. is done under colour of his office - an off-duty police officer does not have the right to search a house and right to private defence is available against him. A police officer carrying out a search without a written authority, cannot be said to be acting under colour of his office. If the act of a public servant is ultra vires, the right of private defence may be exercised against him.

   2. the act does not cause the apprehension of death or grievous hurt - for example, a police man beating a person senselessly can cause apprehension of grievous hurt and the person has the right of private defence against the policeman.

   3. is done under good faith - there must be a reasonable cause of action on part of the public servant. For example, a policeman cannot just pick anybody randomly and put him in jail as a suspect for a theft. There must be some valid ground upon which he bases his suspicion.

   4. the act is not wholly unjustified - The section clearly says that the act may not be strictly justified by law, which takes care of the border line cases where it is not easy to determine whether an act is justified by law. It clearly excludes the acts that

are completely unjustified. For example, if a policeman is beating a person on the street on mere suspicion of theft, his act is clearly unjustified, and the person has the right to defend himself.

However, this right is curtailed only if the person knows or has reasons to believe that the act is being done by a public servant. For example, if A tries to forcibly evict B from an illegally occupied premises, and if B does not know and neither does he have any reason to believe that A is a public servant or that A is acting of the direction of an authorized public servant, B has the right to private defence.

In **Kanwar Singh's case 1965**, a team organized by the municipal corporation was trying to round up stray cattle and was attacked by the accused. It was held that the accused had no right of private defence against the team.

2. when the force applied during the defence exceeds what is required to for the purpose of defence. For example, if A throws a small pebble at B, B does not have the right to shoot A. Or if A, a thief, is running back leaving behind the property that he tried to steal, B does not have the right to shoot A because the threat posed by A has already subsided.

3. In many situations it is not possible to accurately determine how much force is required to repel an attack and thus it is a question of fact and has to be determined on a case-by-case basis whether the accused was justified in using the amount of force that he used and whether he exceeded his right to private defence.

4. In **Kurrim Bux's case 1865**, a thief was trying to enter a house through a hole in the wall. The accused pinned his head down while half of his body was still outside the house. The thief

died due to suffocation. It was held that the use of force by the accused was justified.

5. However, in **Queen vs Fukira Chamar**, in a similar situation, a thief was hit on his head by a pole five times because of which he died. It was held that excessive force was used than required.

6. when it is possible to approach proper authorities - No man has the right to take the law into his hands and so when he has the opportunity to call proper authorities, he does not have the right to private defence. It usually happens when there is a definite information about the time and place of danger. But law does not expect that a person must run away to call proper authorities. The question whether a person has enough time depends on the factors such as -

1. the antecedent knowledge of the attack.
2. how far the information is reliable and precise.
3. the opportunity to give the information to the authorities.
4. the proximity of the police station.

In **Ajodhya Prasad vs State of UP 1924**, the accused received information that they were going to get attacked by some sections of the village. However, they decided that if they separated to report this to the police, they will be in more danger of being pursued and so they waited together. Upon attack, they defended themselves and one of the attackers was killed. It was held that they did not exceed the right of private defence.

(1) Acts of public servants. -There is no right of private defence if the act is done by a public servant if following conditions are fulfilled—

(1) Act must be done or attempted to be done by a public servant;

(2) Act must be done in good faith;

(3) Act must be done by a public servant **under the colour of his office**;
(4) Act must be such as does not cause reasonable apprehension of death or of grievous hurt;
(5) Act may not be strictly justifiable by law; and
(6) There must also be reasonable grounds and or believing that the act was done by public servant as such or under his authority.
This section and Section 99 combined together deal with the right of private defence. The right of private defence is available of person and property, not necessarily one's own person or property but also the person and property of others. In our country, the person has the right to defend mainly his own body and the body of any other person against any offence affecting the human body and property, movable or immovable, of himself or of another against theft, robbery, mischief or criminal trespass or attempt to commit any of these offences. Dacoity is only an aggravated form of robbery and is therefore not expressly mentioned but it was necessary to mention robbery beside theft as it includes extortion.

In the case of State of M.P. v. Mohan Das, father of the accused was trying to pull out the gate of the deceased threshing mill and on the deceased assaulting him in the protection of accused struck him dead. It was held that the right of private defence was not available in these circumstances.

Section 98. Right of private defence against the act of a person of unsound mind. –
When an act, which would otherwise be a certain offence, is not that offence, by reason of the youth, the want of maturity of understanding, unsoundness of mind or the intoxication of the person doing that act, or by reason of any misconception on the part of that person, every person has the same right of private

defence against that act which he would have if the act were that offence.

This principle says that the right of private defence is not dependent on the criminality of the aggressor but on the wrongful character of the act attempted. If an act is not punishable for lack of mens rea, the right of private defence is also available against that act.

Example. –

(a) Z, under the influence of madness, attempts to kill A. Z is guilty of no offence. But A has the same right of private defence which he would have if Z were sane.

(b) A enters by night a house which he is legally entitled to enter. Z, in good faith, taking A for a house breaker attacks A. Here Z by attacking A under this misconception, commits no offence. But A has the same right of private defence against Z, which he would have if Z were not acting under that misconception.

Section 99. Acts against which there is no right of private defence. –

There is no right of private defence against an act which does not reasonably cause the apprehension of death or of grievous hurt, if done, or attempted to be done by a public servant acting in good faith under colour of his office, though that act may not be justifiable by law.

There is no right of private defence against an act which does not reasonably cause the apprehension of death or of grievous hurt, if done, or attempted to be done, by the direction of 8 public servant acting in good faith under colour of his office, though that direction may not be strictly justifiable by law.

There is no right of private defence in cases in which there is time to have recourse to the protection of the public authorities.

Extent to which the right may be exercised. -The right of private defence in no case extends to the inflicting of more harm than it is necessary to inflict for the purpose of defence.

In State of M.P. v. Mishri Lal, there was firing between prosecution party and accused party. Father of one of the accused received five injuries which were dangerous to his life. His son apprehending danger to the life of his father fired gunshot at that point of time in self-defence. It was held that in these circumstances the accused cannot be said to have exceeded his right of private defence.

Explanation 1. -A person is not deprived of the right of private defence against an act done, or attempted to be done, by a public servant, as such, unless he knows or has reason to believe that the person doing the act is such public servant.

Explanation 2. -A person is not deprived of the right of private defence against an act done, or attempted to be done, by the direction of a public servant, unless he knows, or has reason to believe, that the person doing that act is acting by such direction, or unless such person states the authority under which he acts, or if he has authority in writing, unless he produces, such authority, if demanded.

INGREDIENTS

Act of public servants. -There is no right of private defence against an act done by a public servant if the following conditions are fulfilled -

1. Act must be done or attempted to be done by a public servant;
2. Act must be done in good faith;
3. Act must be done by the public servant under colour of his office;

4. Act must be such as does not cause reasonable apprehension of death or of grievous hurt;

5. Act may not be strictly justifiable by law; and

6. There must also be reasonable grounds for believing that the act was done by public servant as such or under his authority.

Acts done under the direction of a public servant. -There is no right of private defence against an act done, by any person under the direction of a public servant if the following conditions are fulfilled -

1. Act must be done or attempted to be done by the direction of a public servant;

2. Act must be done in good faith;

3. Such public servant must be acting under the colour of his office;

4. The Act must be such as does not cause reasonable apprehension of death or of grievous hurt;

5. The direction may not be strictly justifiable by law; and

6. There must be reasonable grounds for believing that the acts were done by

the direction of the public servant or the person acting under the direction must state the authority under which he acts or if he has the authority in writing he must produce it on demand.

Right of private defence of body (100 to 102)

Section 100. When the right of private defence of the body extends to causing death. -

The right of private defence of the body extends, under the restrictions mentioned in the last preceding section, to the voluntary causing of death or of any other harm to the assailant, if the offence which occasions the exercise of the right be of any of the description hereinafter enumerated, namely -

First. -Such an assault as may reasonably cause apprehension that death will otherwise be the consequence of such assault;

Secondly. -Such an assault as may reasonably cause the apprehension that grievous hurt will otherwise be the consequence of such assault;

Thirdly. -An assault with the intention of committing death;

Fourthly. -An assault with the intention of gratifying unnatural lust;

Fifthly. -An assault with the intention of kidnapping or abducting;

Sixthly. -4n assault with the intention of wrongfully confining a person under circumstances which may reasonably cause him to apprehend that he will be unable to have recourse to the public authorities for his release;

Seventhly. -An act of throwing or administering acid or an attempt to throw or administer acid which may reasonably cause the apprehension that grievous hurt will otherwise be the consequences of such act.

Even though this section authorizes a person to cause death of another in certain situation, it is also subject to the same restrictions as given in section 99. Thus, a person cannot apply more force than necessary and must contact the authorities if there is an opportunity.

VISWANATH VS STATE OF UP AIR 1960,

In this case, when the appellant's sister was being abducted from her father's home even though by her husband and there was an assault on her body by the husband, it was held that the appellant had the right of private defence of the body of his sister to the extent of causing death.

To be able to extend this right up to causing death, the apprehension of grievous hurt must be reasonable.

SHEO PERSAN SINGH VS STATE OF UP 1979,

In this case, the driver of a truck drove over and killed two persons sleeping on the road in the night. People ahead of the truck stood in the middle of the road to stop the truck, however, he overran them thereby killing some of them. He pleaded right to private defence as he was apprehensive of the grievous hurt being caused by the people trying to stop him. SC held that although in many cases people have dealt with the errant drivers very seriously, but that does not give him the right of private defence to kill multiple people. The people on the road had a right to arrest the driver and the driver had no right of private defence in running away from the scene of accident killing several people.

YOGENDRA MORARJI VS STATE OF GUJARAT, 1980

This is an important case in which SC observed that when life is in peril the accused was not expected to weigh in golden scales what amount of force does he need to use and summarized the law of private defence of body as under -

1. There is no right of private defence against an act which is not in itself an offence under this code.
2. The right commences as soon as and not before a reasonable apprehension of danger to the body arises from an attempt or thread to commit some offence although the offence may not have been committed and it is continuous with the duration of the apprehension.
3. It is a defensive and not a punitive or retributive right. Thus, the right does not extend to the inflicting of more harm than is necessary for defence.
4. The right extends to the killing of the actual or potential assailant when there is a reasonable and imminent

apprehension of the atrocious crimes enumerated in the six clauses of section 100.
5. There must be no safe or reasonable mode of escape by retreat for the person confronted with an impending peril to life or of grave bodily harm except by inflicting death on the assailant.
6. The right being in essence a defensive right does not accrue and avail where there is time to have recourse to the protection of public authorities.

STATE OF HARYANA V. KARAN SINGH,

In this case, the Supreme Court held that the mere fact of the accused sustaining some injuries in the course of the same transaction does not make it out conclusively that the accused had the occasion to cause death in private defence.

DHIRIA BHAVJI'S CASE,

In this case, it was held that an apprehension in the mind of the accused that death may be caused by witchcraft is unreasonable and, therefore, there can be no right of private defence.

VISWANATH V. STATE OF U.P.,

In this case, the husband went to his father-in-law house for taking his wife. The father-in-law did not agree to rukhsati and thereupon the husband dragged the wife with a view to take her without her consent. On seeing his sister being dragged her brother Viswanath gave a knife wound on his brother-in-law causing his death. The accused was tried for murder. It was held by the Supreme Court that Viswanath had the right of private defence of the body of his sister against an assault by her husband with the intention of abducting her by force and that right extended to the causing of death.

DHANESWAR MOHAKAD V. STATE OF ORISSA,

In this case, it was held by the Supreme Court that in order to plead the right of private defence the ingredients required must be proved. In this case, the deceased had merely gone to the spot and asked the accused party to get the measurement of land done and tried to dislodge one of the poles fixed by the accused. Hence, conviction of accused under Section 302, read with Section 34 is proper.

AVAILABILITY OF RIGHT OF PRIVATE DEFENCE. –

Arjun v. State of Maharashtra:

In this case, it was held that the right of private defence extending to voluntary causing of death is available only if accused shows that there were circumstances giving rise to reasonable grounds for apprehending that either death or grievous hurt would be caused to him. The burden of proof would lie on accused and he has to place necessary Internal or record either by himself adducing positive evidence or by eliciting necessary facts from prosecution witnesses. Degree of proof, however, is not beyond reasonable doubt but mere preponderance of probability.

To decide availability of right of private defence under Section 100, IPC that a person claiming right may have chance to inflict severe and mortal injury on the aggressor it is not relevant to find out whether the right of private defence is available rather entire incident has to be examined with care and viewed in its proper setting.

DETERMINATION OF EXERCISE OF RIGHT OF PRIVATE DEFENCE. -

Ranveer Singh v. State of M.P.,

In this case, complainant Lakhan Singh's cousin, Pappu had some altercation on 81-5-1990 with Kanthshree sister-in-law of appellant. Due to this incident when on 1-6-1990 morning Pappu was going to answer nature call, he was surrounded by accused appellant Ranveer Singh and his son Mannu *alias* Prithviraj and was thrashed to ground. When he shouted complainant Lakhan Singh with many others reached the spot. Accused thereupon asked his son to bring gun. On being exhorted by appellant his son Mannu fired shot which hit sister of complainant present there and it proved fatal. In trial for murder, accused pleaded that he acted in exercise of his right of private defence. It was held by the Supreme Court that accused had exceeded his right of private defence and was liable to be convicted under Section 304 Part I read with Sections 109 and 34, IPC

It was further held by Supreme Court that whether in a particular set of circumstances, 8 persons legitimately acted in the exercise of the right of private defence is a question of fact to be determined on the facts and circumstances of each case. No test in the abstract for determining such a question can be laid down. In determining this question of fact, the Court must consider all the surrounding circumstances. In order to find whether right of private defence is available or not, the injuries received by the accused, the imminence of threat to his safety, the injuries caused by the accused and whether the accused had time to have recourse to public authorities are all relevant factors to be considered

BURDEN OF PROOF OF RIGHT OF PRIVATE DEFENCE. –

Sikander Singh v. State of Bihar,
Eight persons armed with lethal weapons attacked deceased, Upendra Singh causing multiple injuries to him and to his brother

who come to save Upendra Singh. Appellants pleaded that they acted in exercise of their right of private defence but they could not establish the same. Upholding their conviction and sentences ordered by the High Court the Supreme Court held that the burden of proof of right of private defence lies on the accused, but it is not as onerous as one that lies on the prosecution to prove the guilt of the accused. Further, the number of injuries is not always a safe criterion for determining as to who the aggressor was, the right of private defence lasts so long as reasonable apprehension of danger to body or property continues. It was also made clear that the right of private defence is not a right of aggression or of reprisal. In the present case, it was one of the appellants who had come with a gun and fired at the deceased.

Moreover, all of them were having some weapons, such as spears, farsa and lathi. One of them, Rajeshwar Singh after a verbal altercation with the deceased went to his house and came back with a gun along with other accused persons all of whom were armed. Therefore, it was further held that they did not act in exercise of their right of private defence as they were the aggressors.

Section 101. When such right extends to causing any harm other than death. –

If the offence be not of any of the descriptions enumerated in the last preceding section, the right of private defence of the body does not extend to the voluntary causing of death to the assailant, but does extend, under the restrictions mentioned in Section 99, to the voluntary causing to the assailant of any harm other than death.

The right of private defence of body under Section 100 and Section 101 are inter-connected with each other and must be read together. In case of harm caused by the accused which resulted in the death of the deceased in exercise of the right of private defence, the accused is only required to prove that he did not violate the limits laid down in Section 99 of the Code. If n police man in civil dress lawfully attempted to arrest 'A' and A mistook him for n robber and attacked with excessive and unreasonable force 'A' will be liable for causing injury to police man.

Section 102. Commencement and continuance of the right of private defence of the body –

The right of private defence of the body commences as soon as a reasonable apprehension of danger to the body arises from an attempt or threat to commit the offence though the offence may not have been committed, and it continues as long as such apprehension of danger to the body continues.

This section deals that when the right of private defence of the body commences and till what time it continues. It commences as soon as a reasonable apprehension of the danger starts; commission of the offence is not necessary; there is no actual injury that needs to be received before the right of private defence has been exercised. If a man is preparing himself for seizing a dangerous weapon in such a way that if the right of private defence is not exercised he would get severe injury which would amount to causing death of the person in the ordinary course of nature.

In Naveen Chandra v. State of Uttaranchal, it was held that the accused in such circumstances was not entitled to plead the right of private defence. It was also observed that right of private defence is a defensive right and it cannot be pleaded or availed of as a pretext for vindictive aggressive or retributive purposes of offence.

Right of private defence of property [S. 103 to 105]

Section 103. When the right of private defence of property extends to causing death. –

The right of private defence of property extends, under the restrictions mentioned in Section 995 to evolutionary causing of death or any other harm to the wrongdoer, if the offence, the committing of which, or attempting to commit which occasions the exercise of the right, be an offence of any of the description hereinafter enumerated, namely –

First. -Robbery;

Secondly - House breaking by night;

Thirdly. -Mischief by fire committed on any building, tent or vessel which building, tent or vessel is used as human dwelling or as a place for the custody of property,

Fourthly. -Theft, mischief or house trespass under the circumstances as may reasonably cause apprehension that death or grievous hurt will be the consequence if such right of private defence is not exercised.

    A person may cause death in safeguarding his own property or the property of someone else when there is a reason to apprehend than the person whose death has been cause was about to commit one of the offences mentioned in this section or to attempt to commit one of those offences.

UP VS SHIV MURAT 1982,

it was held that to determine whether the action of the accused was justified or not one has to look in to the bona fides of the accused. In cases where there is a marginal excess of the exercise of such right it may be possible to say that the means which a threatened person adopts or the force which he uses should not be weighed in golden scales and it would be inappropriate to adopt tests of detached objectivity which would be so natural in a court room.

ROBBERY OR HOUSE BREAKING BY NIGHT OR MISCHIEF BY FIRE. -

The right of private defence is available to causing death of the accused when the offence being committed or attempted to be being committed is robbery, mischief or house breaking by night.
Theft. - In a case 'A' entered the house of 'B' at midnight' with the intention of committing theft. 'B' struck him with a lathi and 'A' fell unconscious. 'A' gave him another lathi blow on the head of 'B' causing excess bleeding and his death. Here the plea of right of private defence will not be available to 'A' because the force used by 'A' was very excessive than expected. There was no apprehension of death or such injury which amounts to causing death of 'A'.

Section 104. When such right extends to: causing any harm other than death. -

If the offence, the committing of which, or attempting to commit which occasions the exercise of the right of private defence, be theft, mischief or criminal trespass, not of any of the descriptions enumerated in the last preceding section, that right does not extend to the voluntary causing of death, but does extend, subject to the restrictions mentioned in Section 99, to the voluntary causing to the wrongdoer of any harm other than death

This section is inter-connected with Section 103 and restrictions of Section 99.

Examples. -A sees B trespassing on his land, he fires at B and wounds him. It transpired that B had a right to walk over A's land. Here A by mistake took B to be a trespasser. As such 'A' had a right to cause any harm short of death in defence: of his property. But because it was a simple case of trespass and A had fired. It appears that he has caused more harm than was necessary to defend his property from trespass. Therefore, A would be liable for causing hurt.

NATHAN CASE,

It was held that where the accused had killed a person by exceeding his right of private defence of property his case would fall within the exception 2 of Section 300, IPC and his offence would amount to culpable homicide not amounting to murder.

In voluntarily causing hurt or grievous hurt right of private defence under Sections 101 and 104 will not be available.

BALJIT SINGH V. STATE,

The actual, possession of the disputed land permitted the accused to defend the property from being dispossessed. It was held that in exercise of the right of private defence accused's assault on the aggressors resulting fatal injuries to them would defy the limits of lawful exercise of the right of private defence.

Section 105. Commencement and continuance of the right of private defence of property. –

The right of private defence of property commences when a reasonable apprehension of danger to the property commences.

in case of theft - till the offender has effected his retreat with the property or either the assistance of the public authorities is obtained or the property has been recovered.

in case of robbery - as long as the offender causes or attempts to cause to any person death or hurt or wrongful restraint or as long as the fear of instant death or of instance hurt or of instance personal restraint continues.

in case of criminal trespass - as long as the offender continues in the commission of criminal trespass or mischief.

in case of house breaking by night - as long as the house, trespass which has been begun by such house breaking, continues.

AMJAD KHAN VS STATE AIR 1952,

This is an important case. In this case, a criminal riot broke out in the city. A crowd of one community surrounded the shop of A, belonging to other community. The crowd started beating the doors of A with lathis. A then fired a shot which killed B, a member of the crowd. Here, SC held that A had the right of private defence which extended to causing of death because the accused had reasonable ground to apprehend that death or grievous hurt would be caused to his family if he did not act promptly.

STATE V. SIDHNATH RAI,

the Allahabad High Court held that in a case of recapture of stolen property after an interval of time, however, justifiable cannot be deemed an exercise of the right of private defence of property. What is contemplated by Section 105 seems to be a recovery either immediately or made before the offender has reached his final

HUKUM SINGH CASE,

it was held that against criminal trespass, the person in possession of the property has the right of private defence so long as the trespass continues.

Section 106. Right of private defence against deadly assault when there is risk or harm to innocent person. –

If in the exercise of the right of private defence against an assault which reasonably cause the apprehension of death, the offender be so situated that he cannot effectually exercise that right without risk of harm to an innocent person, his right of private defence extends to the running of that risk.

Example. –

A is attacked by a mob who attempt to murder him. He cannot effectively exercise his right of private defence without firing on mob, and he cannot fire without risk of harming children who are mingled with the mob. A commits no offence, if by firing he harms any of the children.

This section extends to the right of private defence of the body against the innocent persons. The harm caused to the innocent persons must be necessary and not excessive as per restrictions imposed by Section 99.

CHAPTER 5. - OF ABETMENT (107 TO 120)

Section 107. Abetment of a thing. –

A person abets the doing of

    First. - instigates any person to do that thing; or

    Secondly. -Engages with one or more other persons in conspiracy for the doing of that thing, if an act or illegal omission takes place in pursuance of that conspiracy and in order to the doing of that thing; or

Thirdly. - Intentionally aids, by any act or illegal omission, the doing of that thing.

Explanation 1. - A person who, by wilful misrepresentation or by wilful concealment Of a material fact which he is bound to disclose, voluntarily causes or procures, or attempts to cause or procure, a thing to be done, it is said to instigate the doing of that thing.

Explanation 2. - Whoever, either prior to or at the time of the commission of an act, does anything in order to facilitate the commission of that act, and thereby facilitate the commission thereof is said to aid the doing of that act.

Ingredients

(1) Instigating a person to
(2) Engaging in a conspiracy
(3) Intentionally aiding a

Punishment. -

Abetment is an offence punishable under the Indian Penal Code or under any law for the time being in force.

Example. -

A, a public officer is authorised by a warrant from a court of justice to apprehend Z. B, knowing that fact and also that C is not Z, wilfully represents to A, that C is Z, and thereby intentionally causes A to apprehend C. Here 'B' abets by instigation of the apprehension of C.

In the case of Hemant Kumar v. State, it was held that where several persons constituting an offence of beating B some of them were armed with sticks. A was the master who allows C to beat B. A was held guilty of abetting the assault made by them.

Instigation may be made direct or by means of letter.
Where 'B' writes a letter to 'A' instigating thereby to beat 'C', the offence of abetment is complete as soon as the letter becomes known to 'A'. If letter never reaches to 'A', 'B' would be guilty of attempt to abet but not for abetment.

The word 'conspiracy' used in this section is defined under Section 120A of Indian Penal Code which defines that when two or more persons agree to do an illegal or to do an act which is not illegal by illegal means. A mere conspiracy would not amount to abetment. Mere presence at the commission of an offence does not amount to an intentional aid unless it was intended to have that effect.

Whether attempt to abetment is punishable? –

According to Section 40 of Indian Penal Code, the abetment of an offence is a substantive offence within the meaning of Section 40. Therefore, attempt to commit the offence of abetment will be covered by the provisions of Section 511 of the Indian Penal Code.

Emperor v. Faiz Hussein,

A Zamindar rented a house to a police officer who was investigating a case, knowing that the house would be used for torturing a suspected thief. He was guilty of the abetment.

Section 108. Abettor. -

A person abets an offence, who either abets the commission of an offence, or the commission of an act which would be an offence, if committed by a person capable by law of committing an offence, with the same intention or knowledge as that of the abettor.

Explanation 1. -The abetment of the illegal omission of an act may amount to an offence although the abettor may not himself be bound to do that act.

Explanation 2. -To constitute the offence of abetment it is not necessary that the act abetted should be committed, or that the effect requisite to constitute the offence should be caused.

Explanation 3. -It is not necessary that the person abetted should be capable by law of committing an offence, or that he should have the same guilty intention or knowledge as that of the abettor, or any guilty intention or knowledge.

Explanation 4. -The abetment of an act being an offence the abetment of such an abetment is also an offence.

Explanation 5. -It is not necessary to the commission of the offence of abetment by conspiracy that the abettor should concert the offence with the person who commits it. It is sufficient if he engages in the conspiracy in pursuance of which the offence is committed.

Ingredients. –

Abettor means -

(1) One who abets the commission of an offence; and

(2) One who abets the commission of an act 'which 'would be an offence if committed by a person not suffering from any physical or mental incapacity.

Examples -

(1) A instigates B to murder C. B refuses to do 80. A is guilty of abetting B to commit murder.

(2) A with a guilty intention abets a child or lunatic person to commit an act which would be an offence, if committed by a person capable by law of committing an offence and having the same intention as A. Here, A

whether the act be committed or not is guilty of abetting an offence.

Bakhtowar case,

the accused asked a doctor to supply poison as a medicine to her son-in-law it was held the accused was liable to offence of abetment as abettor.

S. 109 - Act Abetted is committed

Section 109. Punishment of abetment if the act abetted is committed in consequence and wherein express provision is made for its punishment. –

Whoever abets any offence shall, if the act abetted is committed in consequence of the abetment, and no express provision is made by this Code for the punishment of such abetment, be punished with the punishment provided for the offence.

Explanation. -An act or offence is said to be committed in consequence of abetment, when it is committed in consequence of the instigation, or in pursuance of the conspiracy, or with the aid which constitutes the abetment.

Ingredients

(1) The act abetted is committed in consequence of the abetment; and

(2) No express provision is made in the Code for the punishment of such an abetment.

Example. –

- A instigates B to give false evidence. B in consequence of the instigation commits that offence. A is guilty of abetting that offence and is liable to the same punishment as B.

AN Desai v. State of Maharashtra,

The commission of the offence of rape was in a hut, then possession of the accused thereof was held to be not sufficient in itself to show that the accused abetted the offence.

Nawabkhan v. State,

The accused did not participate in the act of rape but kept watch while others were committing the offence and thereby aided and abetted the commission of the crime instead of preventing. It was held that he was liable to be convicted under Section 376 read with Section 109 of the Indian Penal Code.

Munnuswamy and others v. State of Tamil Nadu,

It was held by Supreme Court that since this is a case of abetment by conspiracy in which all the three conspirators were present and actively participated when plan was executed therefore, C was guilty of murder under Section 302 and A and B were guilty of the offence under Section 302 read with Section 109, Indian Penal Code.

S. 110 – Act done with different intention.

Sec. 110. Punishment of abetment if person abetted does act with different intention from that of abettor. –

Whoever abets the commission of an offence shall, if the person abetted does the act with a different intention or knowledge from that of the abettor, be punished with the punishment provided for the offence which would have been committed if the act had been done with the intention or knowledge of the abettor and with no other.

This section deals with cases under which the person abetted commits the offence with different intention or knowledge from that of the abettor, the abettor would be punished with the punishment provided for the offence abetted. Explanation 3 of Section 108 and Section 110 of Indian Penal Code should be read conjointly.

S. 111 - Different act done

Section 111. Liability of abettor when one act abetted, and a different act done. –

When an act is abetted and a different act is done, the abettor is liable for the act done in the manner and to the same extent as if he had directly abetted it provided that the act done was probable consequence of the abetment and was committed under the influence of the instigation, or with the aid or in pursuance of the conspiracy which constituted the abetment.

Example. -A instigates a child to put poison into the food of Z, and him poison for that purpose. The child in the consequence of the instigation, by mistake pub the poison into the food of Y, which is by the side of the Z. Here, if the child was acting under the influence of A's instigation, and the act done was under the circumstances a probable consequence of the abetment, A is liable in the same manner and to the same extent as if he had instigated the child to put the poison into the food of Y.

In the case of Girija Prasad, it was held that where the act contemplated and instigated was no more than a thrashing with a lathi but one of the assailants suddenly took out a spearhead from his pocket and fatally stabbed the person who was to be thrashed. The others were not held liable for murder or abetment of murder. This section is based on the maxim "every man is presumed to intend the natural consequences of the act".

S. 112- Cumulative punishment for act abetted and act done.

Section 112. Abettor when liable to cumulative punishment for act abetted and for act done. –

If the act for which the abettor is liable under the last preceding section is committed in addition to the act abetted and constitutes a distinct offence, the abettor is liable to punishment for each of the offences.

Example. -A instigates B to resist by force a distress made by a public servant. B in consequence resists that distress. As B has committed both the offence of resisting the distress, and the offence of voluntarily causing grievous hurt, B is liable to punishment for both these offences and if A knew that B was 11Ey voluntarily to cause grievous hurt in resisting the distress A will also be liable to punishment for each of the offences.

S. 113 Liability for the act different for intended.

Section 113. Liability of abettor for an effect caused by the act abetted different from that intended by the abettor. –

When an act is abetted with the intention on the part of the abettor of causing a particular effect, and an act for which the abettor is liable in consequence of the abetment causes a different effect from that intended by the abettor, the abettor is liable for the effect caused in the same manner and to the same extent as if he had abetted which was likely to cause that effect.

Illustration. - A instigates B to cause grievous hurt to Z. B, in consequence of the instigation causes grievous hurt to Z. Z dies in consequence. Here, if A knew that the grievous hurt abetted was likely to cause death, A is liable to be punished with the punishment provided for murder.

Section 114. Abettor present when offence is committed. –

Whenever any person, who if absent would be liable to be punished as an abettor, is present when the act or offence for which he would be punishable in consequence of the abetment is committed, he shall be deemed to have committed such act or offence.

Ingredients

(1) The nature of the act done must constitute an offence;

(2) The act or offence in consequence of the abetment is committed; and

(3) The abettor is present at the time of commission of the act of offence, though another actually commits the offence.

A well-known case in which this section is discussed is Barendra Kumar Ghosh. Wherein it was observed that when circumstances amounting to abetment of a particular crime have first been proved, then after then the presence of the accused at the commission of the crime must be proved.

Krishnasami Naidu case,

it was held that the offence of abetment must complete by the mere presence of the abettor.

Section 115. Abetment of offence punishable with death or imprisonment for life –

If offence not committed –

whoever abets the commission of an offence punishable with death or imprisonment for life, shall, if that offence be not committed in consequence of the abetment, and no express provision is made by this Code for the punishment of such abetment be punished with imprisonment of either description for a term which may extend to seven years and shall also be liable to fine;

If act causing harm, done in consequence. –

And if any act for which the abettor is liable in consequence of the abetment, and which causes hurt to any person, is done, the abettor shall be liable to imprisonment of either description for a term which may extend to fourteen years, and shall also be liable to fine.

Example- A instigates to B for murder of Z. The offence is not committed. If B had murdered Z he would have been subject to the punishment of death or imprisonment for life. Therefore, A is liable to imprisonment for a term which may extend to seven years and also to fine, and if any harm be done to Z in consequence of the abetment he will be liable to imprisonment for a term which may extend to 14 years and to fine.

Section. 116. Abetment of offence punishable with imprisonment. –

If offence be not committed- whoever abets an offence punishable with imprisonment shall, if that offence be not committed in consequence of the abetment, and no express provision is made by this Code for the punishment of such abetment, be punished with imprisonment of any description provided for that offence for a term which may extend to one fourth part of the longest term provided for that offence, or with such fine as is provided for that offence, or with both;

If abettor or person abetted be a public servant whose duty is to prevent offence –

And if the abettor or the person abetted is a public servant, whose duty it is to prevent the commission of such offence the abettor shall be punished with imprisonment of description provided for that offence, for a term which may extend to one half of the longest term provided for that offence, or with such fine as is provided for the offence or with both.

Illustration. –

(1) An officer was offered by A to take bribes as a reward for showing a favour in the exercise of his official functions. The officer refuses to accept the bribe. A is punishable under this section.

(2) A, a police officer, whose duty is to prevent robbery, abets the commission of robbery. Here, though the robbery be not committed, A is liable to one half of the longest term of imprisonment provided for that offence and also to fine.

Section 117. Abetting commission of offence by the public or more than ten persons. –

Whoever abets the commission of an offence by the public generally or by any member of the class of persons exceeding ten, shall be punished with imprisonment of either description for a term which may extend to three years, or with fine, or with both.

Example. -A affix in a public place a placard instigating a sect consisting of more than ten members to meet at a certain time and place for the purpose of attacking the members of an adverse sect while engaged in a procession. A has committed the offence defined in this section.

Section 118. Concealing design to commit offence punishable with death or imprisonment for life. –

Whoever intending to facilitate or knowing it to be likely that he will thereby facilitate the commission of an offence punishable with death or imprisonment for life; voluntarily conceals, by any act or illegal omission, the existence of a design to commit such offence or makes any representation which he knows to be false respecting such design;

If offence be committed: if offence be not committed. - Shall, if that offence be committed, be punished with imprisonment of either description for a term which may extend to seven years; or if the offence be not committed, with imprisonment of either description for a term which may extend to three years, and in either case shall be liable to fine.

Section 119. Public Servant concealing design to commit offence which it is his duty to prevent. –

Whoever, being a public servant intending to facilitate knowing it to be likely that he will thereby facilitate the commission of an offence which it is his duty
as such public servant to prevent; voluntarily conceals, by any act or illegal omission, the existence of a desi3i to commit such offence or makes any representation which he knows to be false respecting such design;

If offence be committed – shall, if the offence be committed, be punished with imprisonment of any description provided for the offence, for a term which may extend to one half of the longest term of such imprisonment; or with such fine as is provided for that offence, or with both.

If offence be punishable with death, etc. -or, if the offence be punishable with death or imprisonment for life, with imprisonment of either description for a term which may extend to ten years.

If offence be not committed. -or, if the offence be not committed shall be punished with imprisonment of any description provided for the offence, for a term which may extend to one fourth part of the longest term of such imprisonment or with such fine as is provided for the offence, or with both.

CHAPTER 5A. CRIMINAL CONSPIRACY (120A, 120B.)

Introduction –

The provision related to criminal conspiracy given under chapter 5A of the IPC. There was no such provision when the Code was enacted. **It was inserted by the amendment of 1913. Before this amendment there was no such provision which can held liable any person who has made any conspiracy but did not commit the actual offence.**

In Simple word Criminal Conspiracy is an agreement to commit an unlawful act. Under this section agreement is itself a crime. Section 120A of the Code defines the word criminal conspiracy. Section 120A is as follows -

Section 120A. Definition of criminal conspiracy. –

When agree to do or cause to be done -
1. An illegal act, or
2. An act which is not illegal by illegal means such an agreement is designated as a criminal conspiracy:

Provided that no agreement except an agreement to commit an offence shall amount to a criminal conspiracy unless some act besides the agreement is done by one or more parties to such agreement in pursuance thereof.

Explanation. - It is immaterial whether the illegal act is the ultimate object of such agreement or is merely incidental to that object.

So, proviso of this section clearly explains that – Only the agreement to do any offence is sufficient to commit the offence of criminal conspiracy. But if there is an agreement to do an act which is not illegal but it is to be done by illegal means then in such case it is necessary to do an overt act for the commission of the offence of criminal conspiracy.

120B- Punishment. –

Punishment of criminal conspiracy is provided under section 120B. According to this section:

(1) Whoever is a party to criminal conspiracy to commit an offence punishable with

death or imprisonment for life or rigorous imprisonment for a term of **two years or upwards shall**, where no express provision is made in this Code for the punishment of such a conspiracy, be punished in the same manner as <u>if he had abetted such offence.</u>

(2) Whoever is a party to a criminal conspiracy **other than** a criminal conspiracy to commit an **offence punishable as aforesaid** shall be punished with imprisonment of either description for a term <u>**not exceeding six months or with fine or with both.**</u>

Ingredients of Criminal Conspiracy

1. There should be an agreement between two or more persons who are alleged to conspire; and
2. The agreement should be to do or cause to be done –
    1. an illegal act, and
    2. An act which is though not illegal by illegal means.

Husband and wife. -In India, the offence of criminal conspiracy can be committed between husband and wife and they are not deemed as one person but in England husband and wife are treated as one person.

In the case of **_Param Hans Yadav v. State of Bihar_**, it was held by the Supreme Court that it is difficult to support the charge of conspiracy with direct evidence in every case but if the prosecution relies upon circumstantial evidence a clear link has to be established and the chain has to be completed otherwise it would be indeed hazardous to accept a part of the link ag a complete one and on the basis of such incomplete evidence the allegation of conspiracy cannot be accepted.

CHAPTER 6 – OF OFFENCES RELATED TO STATE (121 TO 130)

SEDITION

Section 124A. Sedition. -Whoever by words, either spoken or written, or by signs, or by visible representation, or otherwise, brings or attempts to bring into hatred or contempt, or excites or attempts to excite disaffection towards the Government established by law in India, shall be punished with imprisonment which may extend to three years, to which fine may be added, or with fine.

Explanation 1. -The expression "disaffection" includes disloyalty and all feeling of enmity.

Explanation 2. -Comments expressing disapprobation of the measures of the Government with a view to obtain their alteration by lawful means, without exciting or attempting to excite hatred, contempt or disaffection, do not constitute an offence under this section.

Explanation 3. -Comments expressing disapprobation of the administrative or other action of the government without exciting or attempting to excite hatred, contempt or disaffection, do not constitute an offence under this section.

Ingredients

(1) Bringing or attempting to bring into hatred or contempt or exciting or attempting to excite disaffection towards the Government of India; and

(2) Such act or attempt may be done by words either spoken or written or sig1S or by visible representation.

Punishment. -Three years imprisonment with fine or with fine only.

This section came into existence in 1891 by amendment.

In the case of Queen v. Jogendra Chandra Bose, it was held that if a person uses either spoken or written words calculated to create in the minds of the person to whom they are addressed a disposition not to obey the lawful authority of the government or to subvert or resist the authority if and when the occasion should arise and if he does so with the intention of creating such disposition among his hearers or readers they will be guilty under this section.

In the cage of Queen v. Balgangadhar Tilak, it was held that a man must not make or try to make others feel enmity of any kind towards the Government. Amount and intensity of disaffection is immaterial except perhaps in dealing with the question of punishment.

In the case of K.R. Chaudhuri, it was held that it includes the executive power in action and does not mean merely the constitutional frame work.

CHAPTER 7 – OFFENCE RELATED TO ARMY, NAVY AND AIRFORCE. (131 TO 140)

CHAPTER 8 - OF OFFENCES AGAINST THE PUBLIC TRANQUILITY (140 TO 160)

Section 141. Unlawful assembly.

- An assembly of five or more persons is designated an unlawful assembly, if the common object of persons composing the assembly is -

First - To overawe, by criminal force, or show of criminal force, the Central or any State Government or Parliament or the Legislature of any State or any public servant in the exercise of the lawful power of such public servant; or

Second – To resist the execution of any law or any legal process; or

Third. -To commit any mischief or criminal trespass or other offence; or

Fourth. -By means of any criminal force, or show of criminal force, to any person, to take or obtain possession of any property, or to deprive any person of the enjoyment of a right of way, or of the use of water or other incorporeal right of which he is in possession or enjoyment, or to enforce any right or supposed right; or

Fifth. -By means of criminal force, or show of criminal force, to compel any person to do what is not legally bound to do or to omit to do whether is legally entitled to do.

Explanation. -An assembly which was not unlawful when it assembled may subsequently become an unlawful assembly.

Punishment. -Punishment for unlawful assembly is defined under section 143 as - 'Whoever is a member of an unlawful assembly shall be punished with imprisonment of either description for a term which may extend to six months, or with fine, or with both.

Ingredients of unlawful assembly

1. To overawe by criminal force –
(1) The Central Government, or
(2) The State Government, or
(3) The Legislature, or
(4) Any public servant in the exercise of lawful power;
2. To resist the execution of law or legal process;
3. To commit mischief, criminal trespass or any other offence;
4. by animal force -
(1) To take or obtain possession of any property,
(2) to deprive any person of any incorporate right,
(3) To enforce any right or supposed right;
5. by animal force to compel any person -
(1) To do what he is not legally bound to do;
(2) To omit what he is legally entitled to do.

Who will be treated as a member of unlawful assembly? -

Whoever being aware of facts which render any assembly unlawful assembly intentionally joins that assembly or continues in it is said to be a member of unlawful assembly.

In the case of Babu Hamid Khan Mistri v. State, it was held that mere presence in an assembly does not make a person a member of an unlawful assembly unless it is shown that he had done something or omitted to do something which would make him a member of the unlawful assembly or unless the case falls under Section 142.

In another case of Tira Kadu, some persons assembled to prevent a procession by force from passing over a certain street. They neglected the order of the police when asked to disperse, therefore, they were held guilty of being members of an unlawful assembly.

Section 146. Rioting –

Whenever force or violence is used by an unlawful assembly or by any member thereof in prosecution of the common object of such assembly every member of such assembly is guilty of the offence of rioting.

Provision for punishment is provided under Section 147. - According to which whoever is guilty of rioting, shall be punished with imprisonment of either description for a term which may extend to two years, or with fine, or with both." Ingredients. -The ingredients of the rioting are following.

1. The accused persons must be five or more in number and form an unlawful assembly;
2. The accused must be animated by a common object; and
3. The force or violence must be used by the unlawful assembly or any member thereof in prosecution of the common object.

If a number of persons assembled for any lawful purpose suddenly quarrel without any previous intention or design they would not be liable for rioting.

Distinction between riot and unlawful assembly. –

If the parties assemble in a tumultous manner and actually execute their purpose with violence it is a riot or whether they merely meet upon a purpose, which if executed would make them rioters and having done nothing they separate without carrying their purpose into effect it is an unlawful assembly. The use of force distinguishes rioting from an unlawful assembly.

In the case of Raghunath Rai, several Hindus acting in concert forcibly moved some cattle from the possession of a Mohammedan, not for the purpose of causing wrongful gain to themselves or wrongful loss to the owner of the cattle but for the purpose of preventing the slaughter of the cows. They were held guilty of rioting.

CHAPTER 9 - OF OFFENCES BY OR RELATING TO PUBLIC SERVANTS [161 TO 171]

CHAPTER 16 - OF OFFENCES AFFECTING THE HUMAN BODY (299 TO 377)

The word homicide is derived from two Latin words - homo and cide. Homo means human and cide means killing by a human. Homicide means killing of a human being by another human being. A homicide can be lawful or unlawful. Lawful homicide includes situations where a person who has caused the death of another cannot be blamed for his death. For example, in exercising the right of private defense or in other situations explained in Chapter IV of IPC covering General Exceptions. Unlawful homicide means where the killing of another human is not approved or justified by law. Culpable Homicide is in this category. Culpable means blame worthy. Thus, Culpable Homicide means killing of a human being by another human being in a blameworthy or criminal manner.

Section 299 of IPC defines Culpable Homicide as follows -

Section 299. Culpable Homicide. –

Whoever causes death by doing an act with the intention of causing death, or with the intention of causing such bodily injury as is likely to cause death, or with knowledge, that he is likely by such act, to cause death, commits the offence of culpable homicide.

Punishment for culpable homicide is provided under Section 304 of the 12.C.

Ingredients. -

The following are essential elements of culpable homicide -

1. Causing of death of a human being;
2. Such death must have been caused by doing on act;
3. The act must have been done -
    a. With the intention of causing death,
    b. With the intention of causing such bodily injury as is likely to cause death, and
    c. With the knowledge that the doer is likely by such act to cause death.

THREE Explanations provided by section 299.

Explanation 1.

A person who causes bodily injury to another who is labouring under a disorder, disease or bodily infirmity and thereby accelerates the death of that other, shall be deemed to have caused his death.

Explanation 2. –

Where death is caused by bodily injury, the person who causes such bodily injury shall be deemed to have caused the death, although by resorting to proper remedies and skilful treatment the death might have been prevented.

Explanation 3. –

The causing of the death of a child in the mother's womb is not homicide. But it may amount to culpable homicide to cause the death of a living child, if any part of that child has been brought forth, though the child may not have breathed or completely born.

Example –

A knows Z to be behind a bush. B does not know it, 'A' intending to cause or knowing it to be likely to cause Z's death induces B to fire at the bush. B fires and kills Z. Here, B may be guilty of no offence, but A has committed the offence of culpable homicide.

Whoever causes death? -

According to this section, the death means the death of a human being, therefore, child in the mother's womb or unborn child's death does not come in this section. It is not necessary that the person whose death has been caused must be the person to whom accused intended to kill.

By doing an act. -

Death may be caused by any act for example, by poisoning or by hurting with a weapon. Here act includes even on omission of an act for which one is obligated by law to do. For example, if a doctor has a required injection in his hand and he still does not give it to the dying patient and if the patient dies, the doctor is responsible.

The word 'act' used in this section includes illegal omission also. A nurse voluntarily causing death of a child entrusted to her care by omitting to take it out of a tub of water into which it had fallen is an example of illegal omission causing death.

Death may be caused by making some communication to another which caused excitement and death of the listener.

Intention. -

The intention to cause death of any particular person is not necessary. Only intention to cause death is necessary, for example, a person can be guilty of culpable homicide of a person whose death he did not intend. It would be sufficient if the intention of causing such bodily injury as is likely to cause death. The connection between the act and the death caused by the act must be direct and distinct and not immediate it must be too remote.

1. Intention of causing death -

The doer of the act must have intended to cause death. As seen in Illustration 1, the doer wanted or expected someone to die. It is important to note that intention of causing death does not necessarily mean intention of causing death of the person who actually died. If a person does an act with an intention of killing B but A is killed instead, he is still considered to have the intention.

2. Intention of causing such bodily injury as is likely to cause death -

The intention of the offender may not have been to cause death but only an injury that is likely to cause the death of the injured. For example, A might intend only to hit on the skull of a person so as to make him unconscious, but the person dies. In this case, the intention of the person was only to cause an injury, but the injury is such that it is likely to cause death of the person. Thus, he is guilty of Culpable Homicide. However, if A hits B with a broken glass. A did not know that B was haemophilic. B bleeds to death. A is not guilty of Culpable Homicide but only of grievous hurt because he neither had an intention to kill B nor he had any intention to cause any bodily injury as is likely to cause death.

3. Or the act must have been done with the knowledge that such an act may cause death -
When a person does an act which he knows that it has a high probability to cause death, he is responsible for the death which is caused as a result of the act. For example, A knows that loosening the brakes of a vehicle has a high probability of causing death of someone. If B rides such a bike and if he dies, A will be responsible for B's death.

In Jamaluddin's case 1892,

the accused, while exorcising a spirit from the body of a girl beat her so much that she died. They were held guilty of Culpable Homicide.

Negligence -
Sometimes even negligence is considered as knowledge.

In Kangla 1898,

the accused struck a man whom he believed was not a human being but something supernatural. However, he did not take any steps to satisfy himself that the person was not a human being and was thus grossly negligent and was held guilty of Culpable Homicide.

Mohammed's case,

it was held that the act and the death caused should be connected with each other not merely by chain of causes-and effect but by such direct influence as is calculated to produce the effect without the intervention of any considerable change of circumstances.

With the knowledge by act to cause death. -

The accused does the act with the knowledge that he is likely by such act to cause death of the deceased.

Mansel P case,

the accused kicked at the abdomen of the deceased with such violence as to cause fracture of two ribs and rupture of the spleen which was normal. Deceased died. It was held that the accused hew that the abdomen is a most delicate and vulnerable part of the human body and should therefore be presumed to have kicked with the knowledge that by so kicking he was likely to cause death. Sometimes gross negligence may amount to knowledge.

Ganesh Dooley case,

Ganesh Dooley, a snake charmer exhibited in public a venomous snake whose fangs he knew had not been extracted and to show his own skill, but without any intention to cause harm to any one, placed the snake on the head of one of the spectators. The spectator in trying to push off the snake was bitten and died in consequence. The snake charmer was held guilty of culpable homicide not amounting to murder.

Kusa Majhi v. State

The accused dealt blows likely to cause bodily injury which was likely to cause death and dealt blows on the spur of moment and anger. It was held that case fell within the ambit of this section and accused was liable to culpable homicide.

Sobha case,
Accused caused simple injury to deceased, and deceased died of septic which developed on account of the use of wrong remedies and neglects in treatment. It was held that in such a case the death cannot be said to have been caused by the bodily injury within the terms of this section and the accused cannot be held liable for culpable homicide under this section.

Vineet Kumar Chauhan v. State of U.P.,
it was held by Supreme Court that accused at best can be said to have knowledge that use of revolver was likely to cause death and hence he is liable to be convicted under Section 299, Cl. (3) and not under Section 300, I.P.C.

Death of a human being is caused -

It is required that the death of a human being is caused. However, it does not include the death of an unborn child unless any part of that child is brought forth.

MURDER [300 and 302]

Murder is a type of Culpable Homicide where culpability of the accused is quite more than in a mere Culpable Homicide. Section 300 defines the word murder.

Section 300. Murder. - Except in the case hereinafter excepted, culpable homicide is murder if the act by which the death is caused is done with the intention of causing death, or

Secondly. -If it is done with the intention of causing such bodily injury as the offender knows to be likely to cause the death of the person to whom the harm is caused, or

Thirdly. -If it is done with the intention of causing bodily injury to any person and the bodily injury intended to be inflicted is sufficient in the ordinary course of nature to cause death, or

Fourthly. -If the person committing the act knows that it is so imminently dangerous that it must in all probability cause death, or such bodily injury as is likely to cause death, and commits such act without any excuse for incurring the risk of causing death or such injury as aforesaid.

No intention to commit crime. -

State of Rajasthan v. Hukam Singh,

The accused had himself taken deceased to hospital. This by itself indicates that he had no intention result to commit crime and that too, to give gunshot which would inevitably in death of victim. Therefore, the Supreme Court held that the judgment of acquittal of court below was not perverse and, therefore, could not be interfered with.

Significance of motive. -

Abu Thakir and others v. State,
it was held that motive loses significance when direct evidence is available.

Namdeo v. State of Maharashtra:
the appellant, Namdeo and the deceased, Ninaji were residing in one and the same village and relations between them were strained. The reason was that the accused suspected that some

of his animals died due to witch-a-aft played by the deceased. The deceased, Ninaji was sleeping in the backyard of his house. Sopan, son of deceased Ninaji heard shouts of his father calling "Bapare, Bapare". On hearing the cry Sopan and his wife rushed towards the back of his house where his father was sleeping. Sopan saw that the accused was giving axe blows on the head of his father, Ninaji. On seeing Sopan, accused fled away from the place taking axe in his hand. Sopan chased him but could not catch him. The medical opinion was that the injury was sufficient in the ordinary course of nature to cause-death of the victim. The Supreme Court held that considering the nature of weapon (axe) used by the accused and the vital part of the body (head) of the deceased chosen by him for inflicting injuries, it was clear that the intention of the accused was to cause death of the deceased. Therefore, in the circumstances of the case it was covered by Section 300 of Indian Penal Code and not Section 304 of Part 2.

Exceptions - Situations where Culpable Homicide does not amount to Murder

Section 300 also specifies certain situations when the Murder is considered as Culpable Homicide not amounting to Murder. These are -

(Short Details)

1. If the offender does an act that causes death because of **grave and sudden provocation** by the other.
2. If the offender causes death while **exceeding the right to private defense in good faith.**
3. If the offender is a **public servant** and does an act that he, in **good faith, believes to be lawful.**
4. If the act happens in a **sudden fight in the heat of passion.**

5. If the **deceased is above 18 and the death is caused by his own consent**.

Exception 1.

Culpable homicide is not murder if the offender, whilst deprived of the power of self-control by grave and sudden provocation, causes the death of the person who gave the provocation or causes the death of any other person by mistake or accident.

Provisos. -

The above exception is subject to the following provisos -

First - That the provocation is not sought or voluntarily provoked by the offender as a for killing or doing harm to any person;

Secondly. -That the provocation is not given by anything done in obedience to the law or by a public servant in the lawful exercise of the powers of such public servant; and

Thirdly. -That the provocation is not given by anything done in the lawful exercise of the right of private defence.

Explanation. -

Whether the provocation was grave and sudden enough to prevent the offence from amounting to murder is a question of fact.

Illustration –

1. A, under the influence of passion excited by a provocation given by Z, intentionally kills, Y, Z's child. This is Murder, in as much as the provocation was not given by the child, and the death of the child was not caused by accident or misfortune in doing an act caused by the provocation.

2. Y gives grave and sudden provocation to A. A, on this provocation, fires a pistol at Y, neither intending nor knowing

himself to be likely to kill Z, who is near him, but out of sight. A kills Z. Here A has not committed Murder, but merely Culpable Homicide.

3. A is lawfully arrested by Z, a bailiff. A is excited to sudden and violent passion by the arrest, and kills Z. This Murder, in as much as the provocation was given by a thing done by a public servant in the exercise of his powers.

4. A appears as a witness before Z, a Magistrate, Z says that he does not believe a word of A's deposition, and that A has perjured himself. A is moved to sudden passion by these words, and kills Z. This is Murder.

5. 'A' attempts to pull Z's nose, Z, in the exercise of the right of private defence, lays hold of a to prevent him from doing so. A is moved to sudden and violent passion in consequence, and kills Z. This is Murder, in as much as the provocation was given by a thing done in the exercise of the right of private defence.

6. Z strikes B. B is by this provocation excited to violent rage. A, a bystander, intending to take advantage of B's rage, and to cause him to kill Z, puts a knife into B's hand for that purpose. B kills Z with the knife. Here B may have committed only Culpable Homicide, but A is guilty of Murder.

Exception 2.

Culpable homicide is not murder if the offender, in the exercise-in good faith of the right of private defence of person or property, exceeds the power given to him by law and causes the death of the person against whom he is exercising such right of defence without premeditation, and without any intention of doing more harm than is for the purpose of such defence.

Illustration -

Z attempts to horsewhip A, not in such a manner as to cause grievous hurt to A. A draws out a pistol. Z persists in the assault. A believing in good faith that he cannot by any other means prevent himself from being horsewhipped, shoots Z dead. A has not committed Murder, but only Culpable Homicide.

Exception 3 -

Culpable Homicide is not Murder if the offender, being a public servant or aiding a public servant acting or the advancement of public justice, exceeds the powers given to him by law, and causes death by doing an act which he, in good faith, believes to be lawful and necessary for the due discharge of his duty as such public servant and without ill-will towards the person whose death is caused.

Exception 4 -

Culpable Homicide is not Murder if it is committed without premeditation in a sudden fight in the heat of passion upon a sudden quarrel and without the offenders having taken undue advantage or acted in a cruel or unusual manner.

Explanation-

It is immaterial in such cases which party offers the provocation or commits the first assault.

In a very recent case of **Byvarapu Raju vs State of AP 2007**, SC held that in a Murder case, there cannot be any general rule to specify whether the quarrel between the accused and the deceased was due to a sudden provocation or was premeditated. "It is a question of fact and whether a quarrel is sudden or not, must necessarily depend upon the proved facts of each case," a bench of judges Arijit Pasayat and D K Jain observed while reducing to 10 years the life imprisonment of a man accused of killing his father. The bench passed the ruling while upholding an appeal filed by one Byvarapu Raju who challenged the life sentence imposed on him by a session's court and later affirmed by the Andhra Pradesh High Court for killing his 'drunkard' father.

Exception 5.

Culpable homicide is not murder when the person whose death is caused being **above the age of eighteen** years, **suffers death** or takes the risk of death with his own consent.

Illustration -

A, by instigation, voluntarily causes, Z, a person under eighteen years of age to commit suicide. Here, on account of Z's youth, he was incapable of giving consent to his own death; A has therefore abetted Murder.

Punishment for murder (section 302).

Punishment for murder is provided under Section 302 of the Indian penal Code as follows- "Whoever commits murder shall be punished with death, or imprisonment for life, and shall also be liable to fine."

Ingredients

1. Act by which the death caused is done with the intention of causing death;
2. With the intention of causing such bodily injury as the offender knows to be likely to cause death;

3. Injury must be sufficient in the ordinary course of nature to cause death; and

4. Knowledge of imminent dangerous act which in ordinary course of nature cause death.

Important cases.

Amar Singh Munna Singh Suryawanshi v. State of Maharashtra,

The accused, the husband and his wife were living with their children in one room and besides their children only husband and his wife were present in house at the time of occurrence. The husband poured kerosene oil on the body of wife and lit fire was proved. Husband failed to prove as to why he was absconding for about a month after incident. It was held that under the above circumstances husband must be held to be aware that such act was likely to cause death in ordinary course of nature. There was no evidence that the death was the result of accident, Therefore, conviction of accused of murder was upheld.

Ram Adhar v. State of Uttar Pradesh,

The court held that the testimony of injured witness cannot be discarded due to delayed medical examination which was caused due to negligence of constable.

KM Nanavati case.

A well-known case about provocation is that of K. M. Nanavati v. State of Maharashtra wherein it was held that provocation under the Exception 1 must be grave and sudden. The test of grave and sudden provocation as propounded in this case was

(1) Whether a reasonable man belonging to the same class of the society as the accused placed in situation in which the accused was, be so provoked as to lose his power to control himself;

(2) In some circumstances words and gestures may also cause such provocation to control him;

(3) The mental background created by the previous conduct of the victim; and

(4) A fatal blow should be clearly traced to the influence of passion arising from that provocation.

In this case, Nanawati's wife has a paramour named Mr. Ahuja. One day Nanawati sees them during the illicit relationship going on. The accused, a naval officer at that time, knowing the fact went to and asked Ahuja that can he marry with her and answer of Ahuja made him so angry that he killed him. It was held that Nanawati's case does not come within the orbit of this Exception, it was cold-blooded murder.

Sheikh Rafi v. State of A.P. and other,

it was held by the Supreme Court that number of injuries caused though relevant but are not determinative 'Of nature of offence. Nineteen injuries caused in quick succession cannot be as a result of grave and sudden provocation and therefore accused is liable to be convicted for murder under Section 300 and not under Section 304, part 2, I.P.C.

Fakira Chamar case,

A thief was seen with half of his body and head through the wall of a house occupied by women except the accused and his young idiot son and the accused suddenly caught up a rest of pole axe and with it struck the thief five times on his neck and nearly cut off his head. It was held that the accused inflicted more hurt than it was necessary for the defence and was guilty of culpable homicide

Sharad Birdhi Chand Sarda v. State of Maharashtra,

The appellant-accused and the deceased were newly married couple. Nearly four months after the marriage the deceased was found dead on her bed. The medical evidence showed that the cause of death was unnatural. The Supreme Court held that prosecution had failed to prove his case beyond the reasonable doubt as to murder by the accused, therefore the accused is entitled to benefit of doubt. In the absence of evidence -the accused cannot be held guilty of the offence of murder.

Culpable homicide not amounting to murder. -

In the instant case both the carotid artery and jugular vein were found cut and Sultan had soon thereafter lost consciousness. These features are clearly indicative that injury No. 1 was sufficient in the ordinary course of nature to have caused the death. Additionally Dr. Sunder Rajan had. -also stated that lot of blood should have been lost as a result of 16 stab wounds. In our considered view, this is not a case of culpable homicide not amounting to murder. The assault was deliberate and designed to achieve the result namely the death of Sultan, The courts below were therefore right and justified in convicting and sentencing the appellants for the offences punishable under Section 341, 302, 506 (2) IPC. I

Ambit of section. -

In the case of State of Rajasthan v. Arjun Singh, an information was received by Anwa Police that cross firing had taken place between the Rajputs of a village in which Himmat Raj Singh received bullet injuries. In his statement to police the deceased stated that when he was standing outside his house. Arjun Singh fired at him from a muzzle loaded gun from the roof of Karan Singh thereby 2-3 bullets hit him on the left hand and another 2-3 hit his abdomen and; left thigh. His brothers took him inside the house. When they were going to inform police Anwa, Bheem Singh and Gajendra Singh (now absconding), Banney Singh, Karan Singh and Shiraj Singh fired gun shot at them as a result of which both of them received injuries. Thereafter accused Bahadur Singh came with Gandasa. Some women also tried to kill the other family members of deceased with deadly weapons.

Himmat Raj Singh died after 35 days due to septicaemia. Pellets were not recovered either from scene of occurrence or body of injured persons. Gunshot injuries tallied with medical evidence. Dismissing the appeal, the Supreme Court held that non-recovery of pellets cannot be construed as no occurrence of firing as suggested by prosecution to have taken place. Considering the medical evidence that Hemraj Singh sustained seven gunshot injuries which were sufficient to cause death in ordinary course of nature, the Supreme Court was satisfied that death of Himmat Raj Singh, undoubtedly falls within the ambit of Section 302, Indian Penal Code, 1860.

Life imprisonment is the rule and death penalty are an exception.

This Court has time and again reiterated that in criminal jurisprudence in our country, life imprisonment is the rule and death penalty is an exception. It is equally settled law that death penalty can only be awarded in rarest of the rare cases. No doubt each case of murder is gruesome and barbaric, however, the right of life of even an accused has to be respected. In the present case, it is an admitted fact that their existed previous enmity between the families of the deceased and the accused.

The accused were also proved to be from the same village who are neither having any criminal antecedents nor are they history-sheeters. The case is an apparent example of family feud gone horribly wrong. The accused are not posing any danger to society at large. This Court is, thus, inclined that the present case is not within the category of rarest of the rare cases and hence we need not burden ourselves with scaling each and every aggravating and mitigating circumstances. The sentence awarded by the Courts below is adequate for the accused to introspect and able sufficient for the society to heal its wounds.

No interference in acquittal. -

The view taken by the High Court that the chain of circumstances is not complete merely for the reason that drunkenness of the accused is not established, and that the accused cannot be said to have got sexually transmitted disease through his wife, is the view based on irrelevant considerations and could not have been taken in the present case after re-appreciating the evidence on record. It is proved on the record by, Dr. Venkata Reddy that the accused was suffering from balanoposthitis, and Jithuka Nagooru and Jithuka Veeramma have proved the fact that the accused suspected that it might have been transmitted to him through his wife. What is more important is that in. his statement under section 313 of Code of Criminal Procedure when above evidence was put to the accused, he has accepted said fact. What he denied is that he did not go to take his wife to her parents' house. He further denied that he did not take her to night show of any movie, nor committed her murder, in the above circumstances, this Court is of the opinion that in the present case only view possible was the one taken by the Trial Court. As such, it is a fit case where order of acquittal recorded by the High Court requires no interference 2

Entitlement of claim. -In the case of Ramesh Krishna Madhusudan Nayar v. State of Maharashtra, the Supreme Court explained the distinction between Exception 1 and Exception 4 of Section 300, I.P.C. The Fourth Exception of Section 300, I.P.C. covers act done in sudden fight. It deals with a case not covered by the first exception, after which its place would have been more appropriate. The exception is founded upon the same principle, for in there is absence of premediation. But while in the case of Exception 1 there is total deprivation of self-control, in case of Exception 4, there is only that heat of passion which clouds men's sober reasons and urges them to deeds which they would not otherwise do. There is provocation in Exception 4 as in Exception 1, but the injury done is not the direct consequence of that provocation. In fact, Exception 4 deals with cases in which notwithstanding that a blow may have been struck, or some provocation given in the origin of the dispute or in whatever way the quarrel may have originated, yet the subsequent conduct of both parties puts them in respect of guilt upon equal footing. A sudden fight implies mutual provocation and blows on each side. The homicide committed is then clearly not traceable to unilateral provocation, nor in such cases could the whole blame be placed on one side.

In this case, sudden fight or quarrel took place between accused and deceased. Accused thereupon gave two blows by wooden log on the head of deceased. Applying the above principle, the Supreme Court held that the accused under the circumstances was entitled to claim Exception 4 in his defence and was convicted under Section 304, Part I and not for murder.

Conclusive nature of Circumstances. -
It is clear that the present case is based on circumstantial evidence. It is the settled position of law that is a case of

circumstantial evidence the circumstances on which the prosecution relies must be consistent with the sole hypothesis of the guilt of the accused. In case of resting on circumstantial evidence, it is incumbent for the prosecution to prove each and every circumstance on which it proposes to rely. The circumstance so proved should be of conclusive nature, i.e., they should have a definite tendency of implicating the accused. The circumstances so established should form a complete chain which should exclude every hypothesis of innocence and unquestionably point towards the guilt of the accused. In other words, the circumstances should be conclusive i.e., accused and the accused alone has committed the crime.

Sufficiency of Injury in ordinary course of nature of cause death. -

In the case of Atma Ram and others v. State of M.P., accused variously armed assaulted deceased even after he fell down. Injuries caused even on vital parts. Intention to do away the deceased is clear from the nature of assault. It was held that mere fact that no single injury was found to be sufficient in ordinary course of nature to cause death does not alter offence from murder to one under Section 304 Part 2 or Section 326.

Distinction between Section 299 and Section 300 -

Distinction between Section 299 and Section 300 was discussed in the case **of R. v. Govinda**. Fact of the case was that the accused knocked his wife down, put one knee on her chest, struck her with violent blows on her face with closed fist, producing extra variation of blood on the brain and she died in consequence either on the spot or very shortly afterwards, there being no intention to cause death and bodily injury not being sufficient in the ordinary course of nature to cause death. The accused was liable for culpable homicide not amounting to murder.

Distinction between Section 299 and Section 300 are as follows: -

1. When an intention is found to cause death, it would always be a. case of murder unless the case falls within one of the exceptions mentioned in Section 300.
2. All culpable homicides are murder, but all murders are not culpable homicides. A culpable homicide is not murder if the case falls within any of the exceptions mentioned in Section 300.
3. In the offence of murder, the act done by the offender is with the intention of causing bodily injury to any person and the bodily injury intended to be inflicted is sufficient in the ordinary course of nature to cause death but (in culpable homicide, injury would not cause death in the ordinary course of nature.
4. The offence is culpable homicide if the bodily injury intended to be inflicted is to cause death but in the case of murder, such injury is sufficient, in, the ordinary course of nature to cause death.

Murder (When Culpable Homicide amounts to Murder)

Illustrations -

'A' shoots 'Z' with an intention of killing him. 'Z' dies in consequence. 'A' commits Murder.

'A' intentionally gives 'Z' a sword cut that sufficient in ordinary course of nature to cause death. 'Z' dies because of the cut. 'A' commits Murder even though he had no intention to kill 'Z'.

A without any excuse fires a loaded canon on a crowd. One person dies because of it. 'A' commits Murder even though he had no intention to kill that person.

Thus, it can be seen that Murder is very similar to Culpable Homicide and many at times it is difficult to differentiate between them. **J Melvill in the case of R vs Govinda 1876 Bom**. analysed both in the following table -

Culpable Homicide	Murder
A person commits Culpable Homicide if the act by which death is caused is done -	A person commits Murder if the act by which death is caused is done -
1. with the intention of causing death.	1. with the intention of causing death.
2. with an intention to cause such bodily injury as is likely to cause death.	2. with an intention to cause such bodily injury as <u>the offender knows</u> to be likely to cause death of the person <u>to whom the harm is caused</u>. 3. with an intention of causing bodily injury to any person and the bodily injury intended to be inflicted is <u>sufficient in ordinary course of nature to cause death</u>.
3. with the knowledge that such an act <u>is</u> <u>likely</u> to cause death.	4. With the knowledge that the act is so imminently dangerous that it must <u>in all probability</u> cause death.

Based on this table, he pointed out the difference -

when death is caused due to bodily injury, it is the probability of death due to that injury that determines whether it is Culpable Homicide or Murder. If death is only likely it is Culpable Homicide, if death is highly probable, it is Murder.

In Augustine Saldanha vs State of Karnataka LJ 2003, SC deliberated on the difference of Culpable Homicide and Murder. SC observed that in the scheme of the IPC Culpable Homicide is genus and Murder its specie. All 'Murder' is 'Culpable Homicide' but not vice-versa. Speaking generally, 'Culpable Homicide' sans 'special characteristics of Murder is Culpable Homicide not amounting to Murder'. For the purpose of fixing punishment, proportionate to the gravity of the generic offence, the IPC practically recognizes three degrees of Culpable Homicide. The first is, what may be called, **'Culpable Homicide of the first degree'**. This is the greatest form of Culpable Homicide, which is defined in **Section 300** as 'Murder'. The second may be termed as **'Culpable Homicide of the second degree'**. This is punishable under the first part of **Section 304**. Then, there is **'Culpable Homicide of the third degree'**. This is the lowest type of Culpable Homicide and the punishment provided for it is also the lowest among the punishments provided for the three grades. Culpable Homicide of this degree is punishable under the second part of **Section 304**.

It further observed that the academic distinction between 'Murder' and 'Culpable Homicide not amounting to Murder' has always vexed the Courts. They tried to remove confusion through the following table -

Culpable Homicide	Murder
A person commits	Subject to certain exceptions, Culpable

Culpable Homicide if the act by which death is caused is done -	Homicide is Murder if the act by which death is caused is done -
INTENTION	
(a) with the intention of causing death; or	1. with the intention of causing death; or
(b) with an intention to cause such bodily injury as is likely to cause death.	2. with an intention to cause such bodily injury as the offender knows to be likely to cause death of the person to whom the harm is caused. 3. with an intention of causing bodily injury to any person and the bodily injury intended to be inflicted is sufficient in ordinary course of nature to cause death.
KNOWLEDGE	
(c) with the knowledge that such an act is likely to cause death.	4. With the knowledge that the act is so imminently dangerous that it must in all probability cause death.

Thus, it boils down to the knowledge possessed by the offender regarding a particular victim in a particular state being in such condition or state of health that the internal harm caused to him is likely to be fatal, notwithstanding the fact that such harm would not, in the ordinary circumstances, be sufficient to cause death. In such a case, intention to cause death is not an essential requirement. Only the intention of causing such injury coupled with the knowledge of the offender that such injury is likely to cause death, is enough to term it as Murder.

Section 301. Culpable homicide by causing death of person other than person whose death was intended. –

If a person, by doing anything which he intends or knows to be likely to cause death, commits culpable homicide by causing death of any person whose death he neither intends nor knows himself to be likely to cause the culpable homicide committed by the offender is of the description of, which it would have been if he had caused the death of the person whose death he intended or knew himself to be likely to cause.

Section 303. Murder committed by life convict. (Repealed.)

Section 303. - In the case of Mithu v. State of Punjab, the Supreme Court held-that this section is violative of Arts. 14 and 21 of the Constitution and, therefore, unconstitutional.

Section 304-A. Causing death by negligence. –

Whoever causes the death of any person by doing any rash or negligent act not amounting to culpable homicide, shall be punished with imprisonment of either description for n term which may extend to two years or with fine or with both.

Intention is not necessary in this section. Where 'A' takes up a gun not knowing it is loaded, points in sport at B and pulls the trigger B is shot dead. A would be liable for causing the death negligently under this section. Contributary negligence is no defence to a criminal charge.

Section 304B. Dowry Death -

(1) Where the death of a woman is caused by any burns or bodily injury or occurs otherwise than under normal circumstances within seven years of marriage and it is shown that soon before

her death she was subjected to cruelty, harassment by husband or any relative of her husband for or in connection with, any demand for dower, such death shall be called "dowry death" and such husband or relative shall be deemed to have caused her death.

Explanation. –

For the purpose of this sub-section
(1) "dowry" shall have the same meaning as in Section 2 of the Dowry Prohibition Act, 1961.
(2) Whoever commits dowry death shall be punished with imprisonment for a term which shall not be less than seven years but which may extend to imprisonment for life.

Charan Bank v. State,

there was no proof of the harassment. About the expression "soon before" the court said that it is a relative term and it would depend upon the circumstances of each case and no fixed period can be indicated in that regard.

State v. Niku Ram,

it was held that where injuries as found on the person of the deceased (could not have caused her death. the offence would not attract the mischief of Section 304-B though there might have been history for torture for dowry.

Raja Lal Singh v. State of Jharkhand,

it was held by Supreme Court that even if death was by way of suicide, Section 304-B, I.P.C. would be attracted and husband would be liable for conviction under Section 304-B but accused's brother and his wife were entitled to benefit of doubt.

Deen Dayal and others v. State of U.P.

it was held by Supreme Court that words "soon before her death" are to be understood in relative and flexible sense. Those words cannot be construed as laying down a rigid period of time to be mechanically applied in each case.

Dowry death. -

The language of Section 304-B, I.P.C. is unambiguous, plain and simple. For the offence punishable under section 304-B, I.P.C., death of a woman should be caused by any burns or bodily injury or should occur otherwise than under normal circumstances within seven years of her marriage and she should be subjected to cruelty or harassment by her husband or any relative of her husband for, or in connection with, any demand for dowry

Conviction of accused. -

Guru Basavaraj alias Benne Setiappa v. State of Kerala.

The accused was driving tractor. He was driving rashly and negligently. Accident occurred due to detachment of trailer from tractor. It resulted in the death of one and injuries to many others. Accused driver overloaded trailer with goods and also carried many persons. Evidence showed that detachment of trailer occurred as accused moved tractor in speed from main road to kachcha road. Such offence creates stir in society. It creates concavity in social fabric and demands imposition of adequate sentence. Fact that accused was young at the time of accident and had married cannot be a ground to reduce substantive sentence to period already undergone. Further award of compensation under Motor Vehicles Act, 1988 or Section 357, Cr.P.C. cannot be a substitute for sentence. Accused pleaded that accident was due to mechanical failure was not in the circumstances tenable. Hence, conviction of accused was held to be proper, and appeal was dismissed.

Conviction for murder. -

Kuria and another v. State of Rajasthan.

The accused came with weapon to assault. Deceased was first assaulted on road and then taken into the house and, was assaulted again and them thrown out on road. Informant son of deceased had run away on seeing assault. Eyewitness had appeared on scene at that time. Witness was going to his house from bus stand and had stopped on seeing the incident. His presence was natural. Failure of informant to name witnesses in FIR was natural as after coming back at scene and finding his father dead he cannot be expected to view as to who was around. Eyewitnesses' presence at place of occurrence was natural. Eyewitness account was corroborated by inquest report. Post mortem report, statement of investigating officer and recoveries made and blood found on items recovered found to be of blood group of deceased provided motive behind crime. Thus, accused had motive to kill deceased. It is clear case of common intention. Therefore, all accused irrespective whether they have assaulted deceased or not are liable to be convicted for murder.

Case does not fall within the four corners of Section 304 B of IPC. -

Since, as per the information of the doctor, the main cause of death could be the blast of intestinal ulcer and no bodily injury was observed by the doctor during post-mortem examination, Therefore, we find that the case, in hand, does not fall within the four corners of Section 304B, IPC

Sustainability of conviction. -

Ram Pal Singh v. State of U.P., it was held that there is marked distinction between the provisions of section 304, Part I and Part 2 of the I.P.C. Linguistic distinction between the two parts of Section 304 is evident from the very language of this section. There are two apparent distinctions. One in relation to the punishment while other is founded on the intention of causing the act, without any intention but with the knowledge that the act is likely to cause death. Classification of an offence into either part of Section 304 of I.P.C. is primarily a matter of fact. This would have to be decided with reference to the nature of offence, intention of the offender, weapon used, the place and nature of the injuries, existence of the pre-meditated mind, the person participating in the commission of the crime and to some extent the motive for commission of the crime. The evidence led by the parties with reference to all these circumstances greatly helps the court in coming to final conclusion as to under which penal provision of the Code the accused is liable to be punished. This can also be decided from another point of view i.e., by applying the principle of exclusion. This principle can be applied while taking recourse to a two-stage process of determination. Firstly, the court may record preliminary findings if the accused had committed an offence punishable under the substantive provisions of Section 302 of the Code, i.e., culpable homicide amounting to murder. Then secondly, it may proceed to examine if the case fell in any of the exceptions detailed in Section 300 of the Code. This would doubly ensure that the conclusion arrived at by the court is correct on facts and sustainable in law.

Conviction of appellant. -

Arjun v. State of Maharashtra,
The deceased received fatal injuries in fight between accused and deceased parties. Evidence clearly showed that neither deceased nor his wife or son were armed at the time of incident. Accused on the other hand, was armed and gave fatal blow to deceased and caused injuries to his wife. There was no evidence to show that deceased, his wife and son or others attacked accused. Further circumstances do not indicate that there was reasonable apprehension that death or grievous hurt was likely to be caused to accused appellant. Therefore, plea of appellant has no basis and is liable to be rejected. Considering the fact that act was committed in the heat of passion without premediation, and appellant had not taken any undue advantage the Supreme Court converted the conviction of appellant to one under Section 304, Part 2.

Abetment of suicide

The provisions related to abetment of suicide is given under section 305 and 306 of IPC.

Section 305. Abetment of suicide of child or insane person. –

If any person under eighteen years of age, any insane person, any delirious person, any idiot or any person in a state of intoxication commits suicide, whoever abets the Commission of Suicide, shall be punished with death or imprisonment for life or imprisonment for a term not exceeding ten years and shall also be liable to fine.

Section 306. Abetment of suicide. –

If any person commits suicide, whoever abets the commission of such suicide, shall be punished with imprisonment of either description for a term which may extend to ten years, and shall also be liable to fine.

Section 307. Attempt to murder -

Whoever does any act with such intention or knowledge, and under such circumstances that, if he by that act caused death, he would be guilty of murder, shall be punished with imprisonment of either description for a term which may extend to ten years and shall also be liable to fine; and if hurt is caused to any person by such act, the offender shall be liable either to imprisonment for life, or to such punishment as is hereinbefore mentioned.

Attempts by life convicts when - any person offending under this section is under sentence of imprisonment for life, he may, if hurt is caused be punished with death.

Comment -

This means that if a person intentionally does something to kill another and if the other person is not killed, he would be liable for attempt to murder. However, his action must be capable of killing. For example, if a person picks up a pebble and throws it on someone saying, "I will kill you", it is not an attempt to murder because it is not possible to kill someone with a pebble. But if someone swings a thick lathi and misses the head of another person, it is an attempt to murder.

Example. –

(1) A with the intention of causing the death of a child of tender years exposes it in a deserted place A has committed the offence defined under this section.

(2) A, intending to murder Z, buys a gun and loads it. A has not yet committed the offence. 'A' fires the gun at Z. He has committed the offence defined in this section, and, if by such

firing he wounds Z, he is liable to the punishment under this section.

In Sachin Jana and another v. State of West Bengal, accused persons assaulted victim with blows, kicks, iron rods, etc. and poured acid on his face and body and on some other persons. It was held that pouring of acid caused disfigurement and therefore conviction of accused under Section 307, I.P.C. was proper.

Is Injury necessary.

From the wordings of this section, it is clear that a person is liable under this section even if no injury is caused to anyone. However, if hurt is caused, the punishment is more severe. Further, as held in the case of **State of Maharashtra vs Balram Bama Patil 1983,** SC held that for conviction under sec 307, it is not necessary that a bodily injury capable of causing death must be inflicted but the nature of the injury can assist in determining the intention of the accused. Thus, this section makes a distinction between the act of the accused and its result.

Whether act committed must be capable of causing death.

In **Vasudev Gogte's Case 1932,** the accused fired two shots at point blank range at the Governor of Bombay. However, it failed to produce any result because of defect in ammunition or intervention of leather wallet and currency. It was held that to support conviction under this section the accused must have done the act with intention or knowledge that but for any unforeseen intervention, it would cause death. Thus, he was held guilty.

Penultimate Act not necessary

In the case of **Om Prakash vs State of Punjab, AIR 1961**, SC held that a person can be held guilty under this section if his intention is to murder and in pursuance of his intention he does an act towards its commission, even if that act is not the penultimate act. As per **J B K Sharma,** the intention of the culprit is the key and it must be gathered from all the circumstances and not merely from the location, number, and type of injury.

Section 308. Attempt to commit culpable homicide. -

Whoever does any act with such intention or knowledge and under such circumstances that if he by that act caused death he would be guilty of culpable homicide not amounting to murder, shall be punished with imprisonment of either description for a term which may extend to three years, or with fine, or with both and, if hurt is caused to any person by such act, shall be punished with imprisonment of either description for a term which may extend to seven years or with fine, or with both.

This section is similar to Section 307, which deals attempt to murder and Section 308 deals with culpable homicide not amounting to murder.

Section 309. -Attempt to commit suicide -

Whoever attempts to commit suicide and does any act towards the commission of such offence shall be punished with simp1e imprisonment for a term which may extend to one year, or with fine, or with both.

Constitutional validity of Section 309. -In the case of P. Rathinam v. Union of India, constitutional validity was challenged and it was held by the Supreme Court that provision for punishing for attempt to commit suicide is cruel and immoral, irrational and is violative of Art. 21 of the Constitution. It was also added by the

Court that the act of attempt to commit suicide has no baneful effect on the society.

This decision was subsequently reversed by the Supreme Court in 1994 in the case of Gian Kaur v. State of Punjab, wherein it was held that provision for penalising for attempt to commit suicide and abetment of suicide is not unconstitutional.

Section 307, 308, 309 and Section 511

Attempts are dealt with in IPC in three ways -

1. Some sections such as 196 and 197, deal with the offence as well an attempt for that offence.
2. Some sections such as 307 and 308 deal exclusively with an attempt of an offence.
3. The attempts for offenses that are not dealt with in above two are covered by section 511.

Thus, a case of attempt to murder may fall under section 307 as well as section 511. There is a conflict of opinion among the high court's regarding this matter. In the case of **R vs Francis Cassidy 1867, Bombay HC** held that section 511 is wide enough to cover all cases of attempt including attempt to murder. It further held that for application of section 307, the act might cause death if it took effect and it must be capable of causing death in normal circumstances. Otherwise, it cannot lie under 307 even if it has been committed with intention to cause death and was likely, in the belief of the prisoner, to cause death. Such cases may fall under section 511. However, in the case of **Queen vs Nidha 1891, Allahabad HC** expressed a contrary view and held that sec 511 does not apply to attempt to murder. It also held that section 307 is exhaustive and not narrower than section 511.

In the case of **Konee 1867**, it was held that for the application of section 307, the act must be capable of causing death and must also be the penultimate act in commission of the offence, but for section 511, the act may be any act in the series of act and not necessarily the penultimate act. However, this view has now been overruled by SC in the case of **Om Prakash vs State of Punjab AIR 1967**, where the husband tried to kill his wife by denying her food but the wife escaped. In this case, SC held that for section 307, it is not necessary that the act be the penultimate act and convicted the husband under this section.

Section 312. Causing miscarriage. –

Whoever voluntarily causes a woman with child to miscarry, shall if such miscarriage be not caused in good faith for the purpose of saving the life of the woman, be punished with imprisonment of either description for a term which may extend to three years or with fine, or with both; and if the woman be quick unborn child, shall be punished with imprisonment of either description for a term which may extend to seven years, and shall also be liable to fine.

Explanation. - A woman who causes herself to miscarry is within the meaning of this section.

Hurt and Grievous Hurt

In normal sense, hurt means to cause bodily injury or pain to another person. IPC defines Hurt as follows -

Section 319 - Hurt

Whoever causes bodily pain, disease, or infirmity to any person is said to cause hurt.

Essential ingredients-

The essential ingredients of hurt are as follows. -

1. Bodily pain, disease or infirmity must be caused -

Bodily pain, except such slight harm for which nobody would complain, is hurt. For example, pricking a person with pointed object like a needle or punching somebody in the face, or pulling a woman's hair. The duration of the pain is immaterial. Infirmity means when any body organ is not able to function normally. It can be temporary or permanent. It also includes state of mind such as hysteria or terror.

2. It should be caused due to a voluntary act of the accused.

When there is no intention of causing death or bodily injury as is likely to cause death, and there is no knowledge that inflicting such injury would cause death, the accused would be guilty of hurt if the injury is not serious. In **Nga Shwe Po's case 1883**, the accused struck a man one blow on the head with a bamboo yoke and the injured man died, primarily due to excessive opium administered by his friends to alleviate pain. He was held guilty under this section.

The authors of the code have observed that in many cases offences that fall under hurt will also fall under assault. However, there can be certain situations, where they may not. For example, if A leaves food mixed with poison on B's desk and later on B eats the food causing hurt, it cannot be a case of assault.

If the accused did not know about any special condition of the deceased and causes death because of hurt, he will be held guilty of only hurt. Thus, in **Marana Goundan's case AIR 1941**, when the accused kicked a person and the person died because of a diseased spleen, he was held guilty of only hurt.

A physical contact is not necessary. Thus, a when an accused gave food mixed with dhatura and caused poisoning, he was held guilty of Hurt.

Grievous Hurt (320)

Cases of severe hurt are classified under grievous hurt. The authors of the code observed that it would be very difficult to draw a line between hurt and grievous hurt but it was important to draw a line even if it is not perfect so as to punish the cases which are clearly more than hurt. Thus, section 320 of IPC defines Grievous Hurt as -

Section 320 - The following kinds of hurt only are designated as "Grievous" -

1. Emasculation
2. Permanent privation of the sight of either eye.
3. Permanent privation of the hearing of either ear.
4. Privation of any member or a joint.
5. Destruction or permanent impairing of powers of any member or joint.
6. Permanent disfiguration of the head or face.
7. Fracture or dislocation of a bone or tooth.
8. Any hurt which endangers life or which causes the sufferer to be, during the space of twenty days, in severe body pain or unable to follow his ordinary pursuits.

The word 'emasculation' used in this section means depriving a person of masculine vigour castration or making him impotent.

Thus, it can be seen that grievous hurt is a more serious kind of hurt. Since it is not possible to precisely define what is a serious hurt and what is not, to simplify the matter, only hurts described in section 320 are considered serious enough to be called Grievous Hurt. The words "any hurt which endangers life" means that the life is only endangered and not taken away. Stabbing on any vital part, squeezing the testicles, hitting lathi into rectum so that bleeding is caused, have all been held as Hurts that endanger life and thus Grievous Hurts.

As with Hurt, in Grievous Hurt, it is not a physical contact is not necessary.

Difference between Hurt and Grievous Hurt

Definitions -

Only hurts that are defined in section 320 are called Grievous Hurt.

Punishment. -

Punishment for voluntarily causing Hurt as defined in section 323 is imprisonment of either description up to 1 year and a fine up to 1000 Rs, while punishment for voluntarily causing grievous hurt is imprisonment of either description up to 7 years as well as fine.

Difference between Grievous Hurt and Culpable Homicide

The line separating Grievous Hurt and Culpable Homicide is very thin. In Grievous Hurt, the life is endangered due to injury while in Culpable Homicide, death is likely to be caused. Thus, acts neither intended nor likely to cause death may amount to grievous hurt even though death is caused.

Formina Sbastio Azardeo vs State of Goa Daman and Diu 1992 CLJ SC,

the deceased was making publicity about the illicit intimacy between N and W. On the fateful day, N, W, and her husband A caught hold of D and tied him up to a pole and beat him as a result of which he died. They were not armed with any dangerous weapon and had no intention to kill him. N and W were held guilty of only causing grievous hurt.

Section 330. Voluntarily causing hurt to extort confession or to compel restoration of property. -

Whoever voluntarily causes hurt for the purpose of extorting from the sufferer, or any person interested in ' the sufferer, any confession or any information which may lead to the detection of an offence or misconduct, or for the purpose Of constraining the sufferer or any person interested in the sufferer to restore or to cause the restoration of any property or valuable security or to satisfy any claim or demand, or to give information which may lead to the restoration of any property or valuable security, shall be punished with imprisonment of either description for term which may extend to seven years, and shall also be liable to fine.

Example. –

1. A, a police officer, tortures Z in order to induce Z to confess that he had committed a crime. A is guilty of an offence under this section.

2. A, a police officer, tortures B to induce him to point out where certain stolen property is deposited. A is guilty of an offence under this section.

3. A, a revenue officer tortures Z in order to compel him to pay certain arrears of revenue due from Z. A is guilty of an offence under this section.

4. A, a Zamindar tortures a raiyat in order to compel him to pay him rent. A is guilty of an offence under this section.

Wrongful restraint and wrongful confinement.

The provisions related to wrongful restraint and wrongful confinement is given under section 339
to 348. The important provisions relating to wrongful restraint and wrongful confinement are as follows.

Section 339. Wrongful restraint –

Whoever voluntarily obstructs any person so as to prevent that person from proceeding in any direction in which that person has a right to proceed is said wrongfully to restrain that person.

Exception. -

The obstruction of a private way over land or water which a person in good faith believes himself to have a lawful right to obstruct is not an offence within the meaning of this section.

Ingredients

(1) Voluntary obstruction of a person; and
(2) The obstruction must be such as to prevent that person from proceeding in any direction in which he has right to proceed.

Punishment. –

Punishment for wrongful restraint is provided under Section 341 as –

"Whoever wrongfully restrains any person shall be punished with simple imprisonment for a term which may extend to one month, or with fine which may extend to five hundred rupees, or with both."

Section 340. Wrongful confinement -

Whoever wrongfully restrains any person in such manner as to prevent that person from proceeding beyond certain circumscribing limits is said "wrongfully to confine" that person.

Ingredients
(1) Wrongful restraint of a person.
(2) Such restraint must prevent that person from proceeding beyond certain circumscribing limits.

Punishment. -
Punishment of wrongful confinement is made under Section 342 as - "Whoever wrongfully confines any person shall be punished with imprisonment of either description for a term which may extend to one year or with fine which may extend to one thousand rupees or with both."

Distinction between wrongful restraint and wrongful confinement.

Distinction between wrongful restraint and wrongful confinement are as follows: -

(1) In case of wrongful restraint, there is partial restraint of the personal liberty of a person whereas in case of wrongful confinement, there is total or absolute obstruction or restraint of the personal liberty of a person.

(2) Wrongful confinement may be wrongful restraint but vice versa is not possible.

(3) In case of wrongful confinement, certain circumscribing limits are essential whereas in case of wrongful restraint, no such limits are essential.

(4) In case of wrongful restraint, movement of restrained person is obstructed only in one or some particular direction thereby leaving an option for that person to move in any other direction whereas in case of wrongful confinement, movement of confined person is obstructed in all directions and that person is either not allowed to move or is compelled to move against his desires.

Assault and Criminal Force (349 to 358)

The provision related to criminal force and assault is given under section 349 to 358 of IPC. The important provisions related to criminal force and assault are as follows.

Section 349. Force. –

A person is said to use force to another if he causes motion, change of motion, or cessation of motion of that other or he causes to any substance such motion or change of motion or cessation of motion as bring that substance into contact with any part of that other's body or with anything which that other is wearing or carrying or with anything so situated that such contact affects that other's sense of feeling provided that the person causing the motion or cessation of motion causes that motion, change of motion, or cessation of motion in one of the three ways hereinafter described -

First - By his own bodily power;

Secondly - By disposing any substance in such a manner that the motion or change or cessation of motion take place without any further act on the part of any other person; and

Thirdly. -By inducing any animal to move, to change its motion, or to cease to move.

Section 350. Criminal Force. -

Whoever intentionally uses force to any person without that person's consent, in order to the committing of offence, or intending by the use of such force to cause, or knowing it to be likely that by use of such force he will cause injury, fear or annoyance to the person to whom the force is used, is said to use criminal force her.

Ingredients of Criminal Force

(1) Intentional use of force to any person;
(2) Such force should have been used without the consent of the victim; and
(3) The force must have been used to commit an offence or with intention to cause injury, fear or annoyance to the person to whom it is used.

Illustration.

1. 'A' intentionally pulls up a woman's veil. Here, 'A' intentionally uses force to her and if he does so without her consent intending or knowing it to be likely that he may thereby injure, frighten or annoy her he has used criminal force to her.
2. A incites a dog to spring upon Z, without Z's, consent. Here if A intends to cause injury, fear or annoyance to Z, he uses criminal force to Z.

Section 351. Assault. –

Whoever makes any gesture, or any preparation intending or knowing it to be likely that such gesture or preparation will cause any person present to apprehend that he who makes that gesture or preparation is about to use criminal force to that person, is said to commit an assault.

Explanation. -Mere words do not amount to an assault. But the words which a person uses may give to his gesture or preparation such a meaning as may make ' those gestures or preparations amount to an assault.

Punishment. –

Punishment for assault is provided under Section 352, I.P.C. That is imprisonment of either description for a term which may extend to three months or with fine which may extend up to five hundred rupees or with both.

Ingredients of Section 351

(1) Making of any gesture or preparation by a person in the presence of another; and

(2) Intention or knowledge of likelihood that such gesture or preparation will cause the person present to apprehend that the person making it is about to use criminal force to him.

Birbal Khalifa case,

a person took a lathi and shouted that he will break the head of a police officer if he insists upon taking his thumb impression. He was not guilty of assault.

Distinction between assault and criminal force is as follows:

(1) In every use of criminal force assault is included but in case of assault, there is merely apprehension of use of force but there is no use of actual force.

(2) In case of assault, the assaulter or accused must be having enough means and capacity to carry his threat into effect and must also cause an apprehension in the mind of assaulted person that he was about to use criminal force but actually there is no use of such criminal force whereas in case of criminal force, the assault is consummated because, force is actually used.

(3) Assault is something less than criminal force.

(4) In case of assault, the force is cut short before the blow actually falls upon the victim whereas in case of criminal force, force is actually used.

Kidnapping and Abduction

Kidnapping

Kidnapping from India.

Kidnapping from India means taking anybody, without his consent, out of the borders of India. Section 360 defines it as follows -

Section 360 – Kidnaping from India.

Whoever conveys any person beyond the limits of India without the consent of that person or of some person legally authorized to consent on behalf of that person, is said to kidnaps that person from India.

ILLUSTRATION -

If A takes B without his consent or without B's lawful guardians' consent to Pakistan, A would be committing this offence.

Essential Ingredients.

The essential ingredients of Kidnapping are -

(1) The person should be conveyed out of the borders of India.
(2) The person should be conveyed without his consent or without the consent of the person who is legally authorized to consent on his behalf.

Thus, if a person is not capable of giving valid consent as in the case of a minor or a person with unsound mind, the consent of his lawful guardian is required to take him outside India.

Kidnapping from Lawful guardianship -

Kidnapping from lawful guardianship means taking a child away from his lawful guardian without the guardian's consent. Section 361 defines it as follows -

Section 361 - Kidnapping from Lawful guardianship.

Whoever takes or entices any minor under 16 yrs of age if male or 18 yrs of age if female, or any person of unsound mind, out of the keeping of the lawful guardian of such minor or person of unsound mind, without the consent of such guardian, is said to kidnap such minor or person from lawful guardianship.

EXPLANATION -

The words lawful guardian in this section includes any person lawfully entrusted with the care or custody of such minor or other person.

EXCEPTION -

This section does not extend to the act of any person who in good faith believes himself to be the father of an illegitimate child or who in good faith believes himself to be entitled to the lawful custody of such child, unless such act is committed for an immoral or unlawful purpose.

Essential ingredients.

Based on this section the essential ingredients are -

1. The person should either be a minor or a person of unsound mind -

This implies that the person is not capable of giving consent. In case of male child, the age is 16 yrs while in case of a female child the age is 18 yrs. For a person on unsound mind, age is immaterial.

2. Such person be taken or enticed away -

This means that either force is used or any enticement that causes the person to leave domain of the lawful guardian is used. For example, if A shows toffee to a child C thereby causing the child to come out of the house and follow A, it falls under this category.

3. Such person must be taken or enticed away from the lawful guardian -

Only when the child is under the lawful guardian, can he be kidnapped. This means that the child should be under the domain of the lawful guardian. For example, an orphan wandering on the streets cannot be kidnapped because he doesn't have a lawful guardian. However, this does not mean that a child must be with the lawful guardian.

For example, a child siting in a school is also under the dominion of his father and if A takes such a child away, it would be kidnapping. Further, a **lawful guardianship does not necessarily mean a legal guardian.** A legal guardian may entrust the custody of his child to someone else. Taking a child away from such custody will also fall under this section. For example, A entrusts his child to B, his servant, to take the child to school. If, C takes the child away from the servant, this would be kidnapping because the servant has the lawful guardianship of the child.

Section 363. Punishment. –

Whoever kidnaps any person from India or from lawful guardianship, shall be punished with imprisonment of either description for a term which may extend to seven years and shall also be liable to fine.

Varadrajan v. State of Madras,

a minor girl knowingly left the protection of her father and voluntarily joined the accused. The Supreme Court held that the accused have not taken her from the keeping of her lawful guardianship but something more, there was some kind of inducement held out by the accused person so that the minor girl joins with him.

Rekha Rai case,
accused enticed a minor girl to come out of the terrace to the road and then to the motor car in which other co-accused was sitting so that he may drive away with her. It was held that offence of kidnapping was complete only when he drove away with her.

Nur Kadir v. Zulekha Bibi,
Under the Mohammedan law if a Sunni father takes away a son under seven years or a daughter before she attains puberty or an illegitimate child from the custody of the mother he would be guilty under this section because mother is the lawful guardian.

Under the Sunni law, in the case of daughter, mother is lawful guardian until she attains the puberty which is presumed when the daughter completes her age of 15 years and in case of son, not less than seven years.

Bhungee Ahur case,
it was held that taking or enticing a minor out of the keeping of the lawful guardian must be without his consent. The consent of minor is immaterial because minor has no ability to give his consent.

Where paternal uncle's son of a minor girl took her away from the custody of her brother's widow for the purpose of giving her in marriage, it was held that -such relationship would not be a defence to charge of kidnapping a minor from the custody of a de facto guardian.

Distinction between taken away and allowing a child to follow -

In Varadrajan vs State of Madras AIR 1965,

SC observed that there is a difference between taking away a minor and allowing the minor to follow. If a person knowingly does an act which he has reason to believe will cause the child to leave the guardian, then it would amount to taking away the child, however, if child follows a person even when a person does not do any act meant to entice a child to leave his guardian, he cannot be held responsible. For example, if a child follows an ice cream vendor, without any enticement from the vendor, while the guardian fails to keep the watch, the vendor cannot be held guilty under this section.

In Chajju Ram vs State of Punjab AIR 1968,

A minor girl was taken away out of the house for only about 20 - 30 yards. it was held that it was kidnapping because distance is immaterial.

Kidnapping is complete as soon as the minor or the person with unsound mind leaves the custody of the guardian. It is not a continuing offence. Thus, when a child is kidnapped from place P1 and taken to place P2 and then from P2 to P3, kidnapping was done only once.

Abduction (362)

Section 362 of IPC defines Abduction as follows -

Section 362 -

Whoever by force compels, or by any deceitful means induces, any person to go from any place is said to abduct that person. It means compelling a person, or to induce him to go from where he is to another place.

Essential ingredients.

The Essential ingredients are —

1. A person goes from one place to another.
2. Either by forcible compulsion or by inducement.

A person goes from one place to another -

A person cannot be abducted at the same place where he is. For abduction to take place, the person should physically move from one place to another.

Either by forcible compulsion or by inducement -

The movement of the person must be because of some compulsion or because of some inducement. For example, A threatens B on gun point to go from his house to another city. Here, A has compelled B to go from his house and is thus guilty under this section.

Here, the age of the abducted person is immaterial. Thus, even a major can be abducted if he is forced to go from one location. But if a minor is abducted, it may amount to Kidnapping as well. Further, it is a continuing offence. As long as a person is forced to go from place to place, abduction continues.

Abduction is a continuing offence therefore, when a person moves from one place to another will be liable under this section as well as those who involved in subsequently moving are also liable.

In the case of Natha Singh, it was held that if a married woman consents to her own abduction and consent is a free consent, the offence of abduction is not constituted, and the woman would not be liable to abet her own abduction.

Differences among Kidnapping from India, Kidnapping from lawful guardian, and Abduction -

Kidnapping from India (Section 360)	Kidnapping from lawful guardian (Section 361)	Abduction (Section 362)
A person is taken out of the limits of India.	A person is taken away from the lawful guardian.	A person is compelled by force or induced by deception to go from any place.
Age of the person is immaterial.	The person must be less than 16 yrs of age if male, less than 18 if female, or of unsound mind.	Age of the person is immaterial.
It is not a continuing offence.	It is not a continuing offence.	It is a continuing offence.
The person is conveyed without his consent.	Consent of the person kidnapped is immaterial.	Person moves without his consent or the consent is obtained by deceitful means.
It can be done without use of force.	It can be done without use of force or deception.	It is always done by the use of force or deception.

Natha Singh case,

it was held that if a married woman consents to her own abduction and consent is a free consent, the offence of abduction is not constituted, and the woman would not be liable to abet her own abduction.

Distinction between abduction and kidnapping

The offences of Kidnapping and abduction are distinct in following ways: -

1. Abduction is not a substantive offence, but kidnapping is a substantive offence. Abduction -will be made criminal when it is done with one or all intents specified in Section 364.

2. The offence of Kidnapping can be committed only in respect of minor under the age of sixteen years, if male and the age of eighteen years, if female whereas the offence of abduction can be committed in respect of a person of any age group.

3. In kidnapping, the person kidnapped must be removed out of the lawful guardianship. Therefore, a child without a guardian or an orphan cannot be kidnapped, whereas abduction refers to the person kidnapped. The person abducted need not be in keeping of any body.

4. In kidnapping, consent of the person kidnapped is immaterial because they are not competent to signify a valid consent whereas in abduction, consent of the person moved if freely and voluntarily given then it condones the offence.

5. Kidnapping is not a continuing offence because it completes when a person is deprived of his lawful guardianship whereas abduction is a continuing Offence and the

offence of abduction continues so long as a person is moved from one place to another.

6. Simple taking or enticing away of a minor or a person of unsound mind constitutes kidnapping whereas in abduction force, compulsion or deceitful means must be used.

Section 364. Kidnapping or abduction in order to murder. -

Whoever kidnaps or abducts any person in order that such person may be murdered or may be so disposed of as to be put in danger of being murdered, shall be punished with imprisonment for life or rigorous imprisonment for a term which may extend to ten years and shall also be liable to fine.

Ingredients
(1) Kidnapping or abduction of any person;
(2) In order that such person may be murdered; and
(3) Such person may be disposed of as to put in danger of being murdered.

Example. –
(1) A forcibly carries or entices B away from his home in order that B may be murdered. A has committed the offence defined in this section.
(2) A kidnaps Z from India, intending or knowing it to be likely that Z may be sacrificed to an idol. A has committed the offence defined in this section.

State v. Dale LG Rajasthan,
High Court observed that if the person abducted is done to death, his abductors can be convicted under this section even if it is not known who caused the death. Even they in that consequence are acquitted of the charge of murder.

Ashraf v. State,

the accused persons on the false pretext of repaying money to the deceased, induced him to accompany them to another place and after killing him threw his dead body. It was held that they will be convicted under this section read with Sections 300 and 201.

Section 364A. Kidnapping for ransom, etc.

However kidnaps or abducts any person or keeps a person in detention after such kidnapping or abduction, and threatens to cause death or hurt to such person, or by his conduct gives rise to a reasonable apprehension that such person may be put to death or hurt, or causes hurt or death of such person in order to compel the Government or any other person to do or abstain from doing any act or to pay a ransom, shall be punishable with death or imprisonment for life, and shall also be liable to fine.

At present time this section has -become very important because terrorists use to threaten the Government in order to compel to pay a certain sum of money demanded by them or 'persons' acquittal from jail. Nagappa was under custody of Veerappan and certain demand to Government was demanded by him.

Section 366. Kidnapping, abducting or inducing woman to compel her to marriage, etc. -

Whoever kidnaps or abducts any woman with intent that she may be compelled or knowing it to be likely that she will be compelled to marry any person against her will, or in order that she may be forced or seduced to illicit intercourse, or knowing it to be likely that she will be forced or seduced to illicit intercourse, shall be punished with imprisonment of either description for a term which may extend to ten years and shall also be liable to fine; and whoever by means of criminal intimidation as defined in this Code or Of abuse of authority or any other method of compulsion, induces any woman to go from any place with the intent that she may be, or knowing that it is likely that she Will be, forced or seduced to illicit intercourse with another person shall also be punishable as aforesaid.

Section 366A - Procuration of minor girl. –

Whoever by any means whatsoever,
Induces any minor girl under the age of 18 years to go from any place or to do any act with girl may or showing that it is likely that she will be, forced or seduced to illicit intercourse another person shall be punishable with imprisonment which may extend to 10 years, and shall also be liable to fine.

Section 368-B. Importation of girl from foreign country. -

Whoever imports India from any country outside India or from the State of Jammu and Kashmir any girl under the age of 21 years with intent that she may be, or knowing it to be likely that she will be, forced or to illicit intercourse with another person, shall be punishable with imprisonment which may extend to 10 years, and shall also be liable to fine.

SEXUAL OFFENCES

Section 375. Rape. –

A man is said to commit "rape" if he -

(a) Penetrates his penis, to any extent, into the vagina, mouth, urethra or anus of a woman or makes her to do so with him or any other person; or

(b) insert, to any extent, any object or a part of the body, not being the penis, into the vagina, the urethra or anus of a woman or makes her to do so with him or any other person; or

(c) manipulates any part of the body of a woman so as to cause penetration into the vagina, urethra, anus or any part of the body of such woman or makes her to do so him or any other person; or

(d) applies his mouth to the vagina, anus, urethra of a woman or makes her to do so with him or any other person, under circumstances falling under any of the following seven descriptions: -

First. -Against her will.

Second- Without her consent.

Thirdly. -With her consent, when her consent has been obtained by putting her or any person in whom she is interested, in fear of death or of hurt.

Fourthly. -With her consent, when the man knows that he is not her husband and that her consent is given because she believes that he is another man to whom she is or believes herself to be lawfully married.

Fifthly. – With her consent when, at the time of giving such consent, by reason of unsoundness of mind or intoxication or the administration by him personally or through another of any stupefying or unwholesome substance, she is unable to understand the nature and consequences of that to which she gives consent.

With or without her consent when she is under eighteen years of age.

Seventhly. -When she is unable to communicate consent.

Explanation 1. -For the purposes of this section, "vagina" shall also include labia majora.

Explanation 2. - Consent means an unequivocal voluntary agreement when the woman by words, gestures or any form of verbal or non-verbal communication, communicates willingness to participate in the specific sexual act:

Provided that a woman who does not physically resist the act of penetration shall not by reason only of that fact, be regarded as consenting to the sexual activity.

Exception 1. -A medical procedure or intervention shall not constitute rape.

Exception 2. -Sexual intercourse or sexual acts by a man with his own wife, the wife not being under fifteen years of age, is not rape.

INGREDIENTS OF SECTION

(A) Sexual intercourse by a man with a woman.
(B) The sexual intercourse must be under circumstances falling under any of the seven clauses of Section 375.

(A) Sexual intercourse by a man with a woman.

Ram Kripal, S/o Shyam Lal Charmakar v. State of Madhya Pradesh,

It was held by Supreme Court that in case of offence of rape, penetration of male organ in female organ is a sine qua non which was satisfied in this case and hence conviction of accused of offence of rape was proper.

(B) The sexual intercourse must be under circumstances falling under any of the seven clauses of Section 375.

(1) Against her will.

Clause (1) of Section 375 (new description first of Clause (d)) operates where the woman is in possession of her senses and therefore, capable of consenting. It has been held by the Supreme Court in State of Maharashtra v. M.N. Mandikar, that the right of privacy is included in the right to live as guaranteed by Article 21 of the Constitution and a woman of easy virtue is entitled to privacy as and when she likes. She is fully entitled to protect her person if an attempt is made to violate it against her wish.

(2) Without consent.

Clause (5) of S. 375 (new description five of Clause (d)) operates where a woman is insensible whether because of the influence of drink or drugs or any other cause, or is so imbecile that she is incapable of giving any rational consent. Consent as a defence to an allegation of rape requires voluntary participation, not only after the exercise of intelligence based on the knowledge of the act, but after having freely exercised the choice between resistance and assent.

Pradeep Kumar Verma v. State of Bihar,

it was held by the Supreme Court that in case of a representation deliberately made by the accused with a view to elicit the assent of victim without having intention to marry her, will vitiate the consent given by the victim.

(3) Consent obtained by fraud. -

In a case the accused who was engaged to give lessons in singing and voice production to a girl of 16 years of age, had sexual intercourse with her under the pretence that her breathing was not quite right and that he had to perform an operation to enable her to produce her voice properly. If was held that he was guilty of rape.

(4) Consent obtained by putting a woman in fear of death or hurt. -
The part which prompts a woman to give her consent must be of the kind stated in clause (3) of Section 375 (new description four of Clause (d)) that is consent must have been obtained by putting a woman in fear of death or hurt.

(5) Under sixteen years of age. -
Sexual intercourse with a woman with or without -her consent when she is under 16 years amounts to rape. In a case a girl of-seven years was the victim of rape by her own uncle and apart from her testimony being corroborated by evidence of relatives the medical evidence confirmed the episode, conviction followed.

State of U.P. V, Manoj Kumar Pandey,
the Apex Court held that consent of prosecutrix, cannot be presumed on mere fact that she was more than 16 years of age.

Explanation. -
For an offence under this section mere penetration is sufficient to constitute sexual intercourse.

Exception. -
Sexual intercourse by a man with his wife under 15 years of age is rape whether, it has been done with or without her consent.

Complete penetration essential. -
To consider the offence of rape neither Section 375, nor the Explanation attached thereto requires that there should

necessarily be complete penetration. It is also not a requirement that penetration should be coupled with remission of semen or rupture of hymen, Even partial or slightest with or without any omission even an attempted penetration is enough for purpose of Sections 375 and 376, I-P.C. Therefore, the commission of rape is committed even when no physical injury is caused and no seminal discharge. In the case before us all preparation was made by the accused appellant to ravish the victim girl by –

(a) approaching her house;
(b) Taking her by the hand and leading her into the room of the house;
(c) Out the lamp;
(d) Removing her underwear,
(e) Removing his trousers to a certain extent;
(f) Laying her down on the floor and thereafter
(g) The factums of her feeling pain on her private part;
(h) Attempt to raise a hue and cry and placing of the left hand by the accused appellant in the mouth of the victim girl are all indicators to commission of the offence

Section 376. Punishment for rape –

(1) Whoever, except in the cases provided for in sub-section (2), commits rape, shall be punished with rigorous imprisonment of either description for term which shall not be less than seven years, but which may extend to imprisonment for life and shall also be liable to fine.

(2) Whoever, -

    (a) being a police officer, commits rape –

        (1) Within the limits of the police station to which such police officer is appointed;

        (2) In the premises of any station house; or

(3) on a woman in such police officer's custody or in the custody of the police to such police officer; or

(b) being a public servant, commits rape on a woman in such public servant's custody or in the custody of a public servant subordinate to such public servant; or

(c) being a member of the armed forces deployed in an area by the Central or a State Government commits rape in such area; or

(d) being on the management or on -the staff of a jail, remand home or other place of custody established by or under any law for the time being in force or of a women's or children's institution commits rape on any inmate of such jail, remand home place or institution; or

(e) Being the management or on the staff of a hospital, commits rape on a woman in that hospital; or

(f) Being a relative, guardian or teacher of, or a person in a position of trust or authority towards the woman, commits rape on such woman; or

(g) Commits rap during communal or sectarian violence; or

(h) Commits rape on a woman knowing her to be pregnant; or

(I) Commits rape on a woman when she is under sixteen years

(j) commits rape, on a woman incapable of giving consent;

(k) Being in a position of control or dominance over a such woman- or

(l) Commits rape on a woman suffering from mental or physical disability; or

(m) While committing rape causes grievous bodily harm or maims or disfigures or endangers the life of a woman; or

(n) Commits rape repeatedly on the same woman, shall be punished with rigorous imprisonment for a term which shall not be less than ten years, but which may extend to imprisonment for life, which shall mean imprisonment for the remainder of that person's natural life, and shall also be liable to be fine.

Explanation. -

For the purposes of this subsection, -

(a) "armed forces" means the naval, military and air forces and includes any member of the Armed Forces constituted under any law for the time being in force, including the paramilitary forces and any auxiliary forces that are under the control of the Central Government or the State Government;

(b) "Hospital" means the precincts of the hospital and includes the precincts of any institution for the reception and treatment of persons during convalescence or of persons requiring medical attention or rehabilitation;

(c) "Police officer" shall have the same meaning as assigned to the expression

"police" under the Police Act, 1861;

(d) "women's or children's institution" means an institution, whether called an orphanage or a home for neglected women or children or a widow's home or an institution called by any other name, which is established and maintained for the reception and care of women or children.

376A. Punishment for causing death or resulting in persistent vegetative state of victim. –

Whoever, commits an offence punishable under sub-section (1) or sub-section (2) of Section 376 and in the course of such commission inflicts an injury which causes the death of the woman or causes the woman to be in a persistent vegetative state shall be punished with rigorous imprisonment for a term which shall not be less than twenty years, but which may extend to imprisonment for life, which shall mean imprisonment for the remainder of that person's natural life, or with death.

376B. Sexual intercourse by husband upon his wife during separation. -
Whoever has sexual intercourse with his own wife, that person is living separately, whether under a decree of separation or otherwise, without her consent, shall be punished with imprisonment of either description for a term which shall not be less than two years but which may extend to seven years, and shall also be liable to fine.

Explanation. -on this section, "sexual intercourse" shall mean any of the acts mentioned in clauses (a) to (d) of section 375.

376C. Sexual intercourse by a person in authority. -
Whoever, being –

    (a) in a position of authority or in a fiduciary relationship; or

    (b) a public servant; or

    (c) superintendent or manager of a jail, remand home or other place of custody established by or under any law for the time being in force, or a women's or children's institution; or

    (d) on the management of a hospital or being on the staff of a hospital, abuses such position or fiduciary relationship to induce or seduce any woman either in his custody or under his charge or present in the premises to have sexual intercourse with him, such sexual intercourse not amounting to the offence of rape, shall be punished with rigorous imprisonment of either description for a term which shall not be less than five years, but which may extend to ten years, and shall also be liable to fine.

Explanation 1.-
In this section, "sexual intercourse" shall mean any of the acts mentioned in clauses (a) to (d) of Section 375.

Explanation 2. -
For the purposes of this section, Explanation 1 to Section 375 shall also be applicable.

Explanation 3. -
"Superintendent", in relation to a jail, remand home or other place of custody or a women's or children's institution, includes a person holding any other office in such jail, remand home, place or institution by virtue 'of which such person can exercise any authority or control over its inmates.

Explanation 4. -
The expressions "hospital" and "women's or children's institution" shall respectively have the same meaning as in Explanation to sub-section (2) of Section 376.

376D. Gang Rape. -

Where a woman is raped by one or more persons constituting a group or acting in furtherance of a common intention, each of those persons shall be deemed to have committed the offence of rape and shall be punished with rigorous imprisonment for a term which shall not be less than twenty years, but which may extend to life which shall mean imprisonment for the remainder of that person's natural life, and with fine:

Provided that such fine shall be just and reasonable to meet the medical expenses and rehabilitation of the victim:

Provided further that any fine imposed under this section shall be paid to the victim.

376E. Punishment for repeat offenders. -

Whoever has been previously convicted of an offence punishable under Section 376 or Section 376A or Section 376D and Y is subsequently convicted of an offence punishment under any of the said sections shall be punished with imprisonment for life which shall mean imprisonment for the remainder of that person's natural life, or with death."

Tenability of conviction. -

UTPAL DAS AND ANOTHER V. STATE OF WEST BENGAL,

one Sitarani Jha got down from the train at 8 p.m. on 28-4-1984 and hired a rickshaw for bus stand. On reaching there she found that the last bus had already left. Then she asked rickshaw-puller to take her to a nearby village where her girlfriend was living. When she was about to leave bus stand she was intercepted by four or five persons who forcibly took her to a house under construction and committed rape on her one after another against her will. After committing rape, she was taken to a tea stall and was locked in a small room. After some time, she was rescued by some people to whom she narrated the whole story. She stayed in the night there in the house of her relative. The next morning, the local people brought Utpal Das (Appellant No. 1) and Haradhan

(Appellant No. 2) and Banshidhar before the victim and she identified Utpal and Haradhan as the persons who committed rape. At that stage Hardhan managed to flee away. F.I.R. was lodged at Police Station at 10.45 a.m. on 29-4-1984. A case under Sections 366, 368 and 376 read with Section 34 was registered. Sitarani was the mother of two children. On medical examination no injuries were found on her private parts.

It was held by the Supreme Court that the victim was a married lady with two children, as such absence of injuries on her private parts cannot be ground to hold that stage she was not subjected to any sexual assault. Moreover, married ladies are habituated to sexual intercourse so no injury on private parts can be expected. As far the plea of consensual sexual intercourse is concerned, it was held that the plea was raised for the first time across bar, therefore, it was not tenable. Therefore, the appeal was dismissed.

Legality of conviction of appellant. -

In the case of Ram Singh v. State of H.P., the victim of rape Smt. Chanchala Devi was a midwife by profession. On one night Naresh Singh came to her house and requested her to go to his house because his brother's wife was having labour pains. Initially she was reluctant to go but later on she accompanied Naresh Singh. When both of them were on their way one Ram Singh met them and accompanied them. While all the three were going towards the house of Naresh Singh, Naresh caught hold of the victim Chanchala Devi and the appellant Ram Singh laid her on ground and opened her trousers. When victim tried to raise alarm, Naresh gave a fist blow on her mouth and then gagged it. Both the accused performed sexual intercourse forcibly with the victim and thereafter sneaked away from the place F.I.R. was lodged on 14-8-1989 and the victim was medically examined the same day at about 12.15 p.m. The accused was also medically examined. In view of these facts the accused were held guilty of rape and in appeal the defence counsel pleaded that blood-stained clothes of victim were not sent for chemical examination and that there was no injury on her private parts. To these the Supreme Court holding the accused guilty said that the testimony of victim inspires confidence. Her testimony is not only corroborated by other evidence but also by medical evidence. Further failure of investigating agency to send blood-stained clothes for medical examination cannot be a ground to discredit the testimony of victim. The victim had no control over the investigating agency and the negligence, if any, of the investigating officer could not affect the credibility of the statement of victim. As far as the absence of injury on private parts is concerned, the doctor has found that the prosecutrix was used to sexual intercourse and as such absence of injury on the private parts of the victim may not be very significant. Therefore, the conviction of appellant for committing rape is quite justified being based on evidence on record.

Need of corroboration of testimony of prosecutrix. -

O.M. Baby (dead) by L.R.'s v. State of Kerala,

There was contradictory report of vaginal swab and smear. First report showed absence of sperm. Second report obtained on the basis of medical examination done a few days after the incident gave contradictory results. Such report obtained on application made to Magistrate doubting fairness of first examination. There was clear evidence of Doctor that sperms remain in vaginal canal for 17 days. Second report as such cannot be ignored. Testimony of prosecutrix corroborated by external injuries found on her body. Absence of injuries or marks of violence on the person of prosecutrix is not decisive, particularly when the victim did not offer any resistance on account of threat or fear. It was held by the Supreme Court that testimony of prosecutrix cannot be ignored for Want, of corroboration unless inconsistencies or contradictions are sufficiently serious. Considering prevailing conditions in country woman would not come with false case of sexual assault and this fact has to be kept in mind while appreciating evidence. Considering the entire evidence on record accused was liable to be convicted.

Acquittal of accused of gang rape. -

In the case of State of Rajasthan v. Hanif Khan and another, accused persons, allegedly gang raped the victim and threw her into a pit when they found her dead. Eye-witness wife of accused revealed the incident but her evidence was discarded by the High Court without any discussion. The complainant father of victim was not an eyewitness. It 'was held by the Supreme Court that the fact' that complainant had not indicated in complaint as to what the eyewitness had told him cannot be a ground to discard her evidence. The reasoning of the High Court was wrong and showed total non-application of mind. Therefore, acquittal of accused was held to be improper.

Joint liability for gang rape. -

Om Prakash v. State of Haryana,

is a case relating to gang rape? In this case, accused alone at knife point kidnapped prosecutrix and appellant only provided space and cot and helped co-accused in wrongfully detaining prosecutrix. There was no evidence to show that the factum of kidnapping as well as extent to commit rape was known to appellant.

In view of the statement of prosecutrix, the act of kidnapping and actual commission of rape was completed by co-accused himself. There is no evidence that there was common concert or common intention or meeting of minds prior to commission of offence between the two accused which is necessary under Section 376(2)(g). Therefore, conviction of accused under Section 376(2)(g) was set aside. However, conviction under Section 368 1.P. Code was maintained.

It was made clear by the Supreme Court that for offence under Section 376(2)(g), the act has to be in furtherance of common intention of each of the persons. This provision embodies a principle of joint liability and essence of that liability is existence of common intention and that common intention presupposes prior concert which may be determined from conduct of offenders which is revealed during the course of action.

of Unnatural Offences (377)

The provisions related to unnatural offences is given under section 377 of IPC. Section 377 of IPC is as follows.

Section 377. Unnatural offences. -

Whoever voluntarily has carnal intercourse against the order of nature with any man, woman or animal, shall be punished with imprisonment for life, or with imprisonment of either description for a term which may extend to 10 years, and shall also be liable to fine.

Explanation. -

Penetration is sufficient to constitute the carnal intercourse necessary to the offence described in this Section.

The accused was charged for committing an unnatural offence upon a young boy. In view of the fact that no force was used, the sentence of 3 years' imprisonment was reduced to 6 months. It was held that in judging the depravity of the action for determining quantum of sentence, all aspects of the matter having a bearing on the question of nature of offence must be considered.

Difference between rape and adultery.

Difference between rape and adultery is as follows: -

(1) Rape is an offence against the woman herself whereas adultery is an offence against the husband.

(2) Rape is defined under Section 376 of the IPC under Chapter titled "The Offences Against the Human Body" and is an offence regarding the person of the woman who is victim of rape whereas adultery is an offence defined under Section 397 of the IPC ' and it is an offence relating to marriage.

(3) Offence of rape is committed against the will and without consent of the woman or it may be committed even with the consent if the victim girl is under 16 years of the age whereas in case of adultery, the consent of the woman is not essential as the woman being married it is the husband who is actually the aggrieved party.

(4) Rape may be committed on any woman whether married or unmarried. If the woman is married and sexual intercourse is committed without her consent, the offence is said to be rape as well as adultery whereas adultery may be committed only if the woman is married and not when she is not married. But no offence of adultery is committed where the husband consents to his wife having illicit relationship.

CHAPTER 17. OF OFFENCES AGAINST PROPERTY (378 TO 462)

Theft, Robbery and Dacoity

Theft (378 to 382)

In general, theft is committed when a person's property is taken without his consent by someone. For example, A enters the house of B and takes B's watch without B seeing and puts it in his pocket with an intention to take it for himself. A commits theft. However, besides the ordinary meaning conveyed by the word theft, the scope of theft is quite wide. **Section 378** of IPC defines theft as follows -

Section 378 – Theft.

Whoever, intending to take dishonestly any movable property out of the possession of any person without that person's consent, moves that property in order to such taking, is said to commit theft.

Explanations.

EXPLANATION 1. -

A thing so long as it is attached to the earth, not being movable property, is not the subject of theft, but it becomes capable of being the subject of theft as soon as it is severed from the earth.

EXPLANATION 2. -

A moving affected by the same act which affects the severance may be a theft.

EXPLANATION 3. -

A person is said to cause a thing to move by removing an obstacle which prevented it from moving or by separating it from any other thing as well as by actually moving it.

EXPLANATION 4. -

A person, who by any means causes an animal to move, is said to move that animal, and to move everything which, in consequence of the motion so caused, is moved by that animal.

EXPLANATION 5. -

The consent mentioned in the definition may be express or implied, and may be given either by the person in possession, or by any person having for that purpose authority either express or implied.

ESSENTIAL INGREDIENTS

Based on this definition, the following are the essential constituents of Theft -

(1) Dishonest intention to take property;
(2) The property must be movable;
(3) The property should be taken out of the possession of another person;
(4) The property should be taken without the consent of that person; and
(5) There must be some moving of the property in order to accomplish the taking of it.

(1) DISHONEST INTENTION. -

There must be dishonest intention on the part of the offender. The dishonest intention is defined under **section 24** of IPC. The intention to take dishonestly exists when the taker intends **to cause wrongful gain to one person or wrongful loss to**

another person. Taking without any dishonest intention is not theft. The intention to take dishonestly must exist at the time of moving of the property.

Examples.

- A sees a ring belonging to Z lying on a table in Z's house. Not venturing to misappropriate the ring immediately for fear of search and detection, A hides the ring in a place where it is highly improbable that it will ever be found by Z, with the intention of taking the ring from the hiding place and selling it when the loss is forgotten. Here at the time of first moving the ring, commits theft.
- A quietly takes money from B's purse for his spending. Here, A causes wrongful loss to B and is thus guilty of theft.

It is not necessary that the taking should be permanent or with an intention to appropriate the thing, taken,

Examples.

- 'A' cuts down a tree on Z's ground, with the intention of dishonestly taking the tree out of Z's possession without Z's consent. Here, as soon as A has severed the tree in order to such taking, he has committed theft. (Illustration 1 of Section 378 of IPC)

Further, a person can also be convicted of stealing his own property if he takes it dishonestly from another.

Illustrations (j) and (k) of the Code appended to the section provide the example. Where a person removes his cattle after attachment from the person to whom they have been entrusted without recourse to the Court under whose order the attachment has been made, he will be guilty of theft.

However, if the intention of the offender is not to cause a wrongful loss or wrongful gain, he does not commit theft even if he takes the property without consent. For example, A gives his watch to B for repairing. B takes the watch to his shop. A, who does not owe any debt to B for which B has the right to retain the watch, follows B and forcibly takes back the watch. Here, A does not commit theft because he has no dishonest intention. Similarly, when A, believing, in good faith, a property in possession of B, to be his, takes it from B, it is not theft.

(2) MOVABLE PROPERTY. -

Only movable property can be the subject matter of theft. Anything which is permanently attached with the earth is known as immovable property. An immovable property cannot be stolen or moved from the possession so a theft cannot happen in respect of an immovable property.

Explanations (1) and (2) make it clear that things attached to the land may become movable property by severance from the earth and that the **act of severance may of itself be theft.**

Explanation 1 - As long as a thing is attached to earth, not being movable, is not subject of theft. However, as soon as it is severed from the earth, it is capable of being the subject of theft.

Explanation 2 says that a moving affected by the same act that causes severance, may be theft.

(3) TAKING OUT OF THE POSSESSION OF ANOTHER PERSON. -

For constituting the offence of theft, the taking of the property must be from the possession of another person. The property must be in the possession of the prosecutor, whether he is the owner of it or is in possession of it in some other manner.

Illustration (g) of the Code demonstrates that where property dishonestly taken belonged to a person who was dead, and therefore, in nobody's possession, or where it is lost property without any apparent possessor, not the offence of theft but of criminal misappropriation is constituted.

A property that is not in possession of anybody cannot be a subject of theft.

For example,

- Wild dogs cannot be a subject of theft and so if someone takes a wild dog, it will not be theft. It is not important whether the person who possess the thing is the rightful owner of that thing or not. If the thing is moved out of mere possession of someone, it will be theft.
- A, a coin collector, steals some coins from B, a fellow coin collector. A find out that they were his coins that were stolen earlier. Here, even though B was not the rightful owner of the coins, he was still in possession of them and so A is guilty of theft.

Transfer of possession of movable property without consent of the person in possession need not, however, be permanent or for a considerable length of time nor is it necessary that the property should be found in possession of the accused.

(4) CONSENT -

The property must have been taken without the consent of the person in possession of it. Explanation (5) of the Code and illustrations (m) and (n) thereof make it clear that the consent may be expressed or implied, and may be either by the person in possession, or by any person having for that purpose authority either express or implied. Consent obtained by false representation which leads to a misconception of facts will not be a valid consent.

Explanation 5, consent can be express or implied.
For example,

- A, a good friend of B, goes to B's library and takes a book without express consent of B, with the intention of reading it and returning it. Here, A might have conceived that he had B's implied consent to take the book and so he is not guilty of theft.
- When A asks for charity from B's wife, and when she gives A some clothes belonging to B, A may conceive that she has the authority to give B's clothes and so A is not guilty of theft.

(5) MOVES THE PROPERTY IN ORDER OF TAKING. -

To constitute theft, "moving of property" should also be established. Merely because some property of A is found in the possession of P would not make P a thief. The Supreme Court said in KN. Mehra v. State of Rajasthan, it is rightly pointed out that since the definition of theft requires that the moving of the property is to be in order to such taking, such taking means 'intending to take it dishonestly' the very moving out must be with the dishonest intention.

Even where a person has an intention to take some property dishonestly the offence of theft will not be constituted unless the property is moved. Thus, mere seizure of cattle found trespassing on land does not amount to moving the cattle. It will be an offence only when they are moved out.

Explanation 3 and 4 of section 378 is related with the moving of property for the purpose of theft.

As per **Explanation 3**, moving the support or obstacle that keeps the property from moving is also theft. For example, removing the pegs to which bullocks are tied, is theft.

Further, as per **Explanation 4**, causing an animal to move, is also considered as moving the things that move in consequence.

For example, -

- A moves the bullock cart carrying a box of treasure. Here, A is guilty of moving the box of treasure.

In K. N. Mehra v. State of Rajasthan AIR 1957 S. C. 369,

SC held that proof of intention to cause permanent deprivation of property to the owner, or to obtain a personal gain is not necessary for the purpose of establishing dishonest intention. Thus, In **Pyarelal Bhargava vs State AIR 1963**, a govt. employee took a file from the govt. office, presented it to B, and brought it back to the office after two days. It was held that permanent taking of the property is not required, even a temporary movement of the property with dishonest intention is enough and thus this was theft.

In White's case, 1853,

a person introduced another pipe in a gas pipeline and consumed the gas bypassing the meter. Gas was held to be a movable property and he was held guilty of theft.

In HJ Ransom vs Triloki Nath 1942,

A had taken a bus on hire purchase from B under the agreement that in case of default B has the right to take back the possession of the bus. A defaulted, and thereupon, B forcibly took the bus from C, who was the driver of the bus. It was held that the C was the employee of A and thus, the bus was in possession of A. Therefore, taking the bus out of his possession was theft.

In Chandler's case, 1913,

A and B were both servants of C. A suggested B to rob C's store. B agreed to this and procured keys to the store and gave them to A, who then made duplicate copies. At the time of the robbery, they were caught because B had already informed C and to catch A red handed, C had allowed B to accompany A on the theft. Here, B had the consent of C to move C's things but A did not and so A was held guilty of theft.

In Bishaki's case 1917,

the accused cut the string that tied the necklace in the neck of a woman, because of which the necklace fell. It was held that he caused sufficient movement of the property as needed for theft.

Theft of one's own property

As per the definition of theft given in section 378, it is not the ownership but the possession of the property that is important. A person may be a legal owner of a property but if that property is in possession, legally valid or invalid, of another, it is possible for the owner to commit theft of his own property.

This is explained in **illustration j** of section 378 - A gives his watch to B for repairs. B repairs the watch, but A does not pay the repairing charges, because of which B does not return the watch as a security. A forcibly takes his watch from B. Here, A is guilty of theft of his own watch.

Further, in **illustration k**, A pawns his watch to B. He takes it out of B's possession, having not paid to B what he borrowed by pawning it, without B's consent. Thus, he commits theft of his own property in as much as he takes it dishonestly.

In Rama's Case 1956,

A person's cattle were attached by the court and entrusted with another. He took the cattle out of the trustee's possession without recourse of the court. He was held guilty of theft.

Section 379. Punishment for theft. -

Whoever commits theft shall be punished with imprisonment of either description for a term which may extend to 3 years, or with fine, or with both.

Extortion (383)

In Extortion, a person takes the property of another by threat without any legal justification. Section 383 defines extortion as follows -

Section 383 – Extortion.

Whoever intentionally puts any person in fear of any injury to that person, or to any other, and thereby dishonestly induces the person so put in fear to deliver to any person any property or valuable security or anything signed or sealed, which may be converted into a valuable security, commits extortion.

For example, 'A' threatens to publish a defamatory libel about 'B' unless 'B' gives him money. 'A' has committed extortion. 'A' threatens 'B' that he will keep B's child in wrongful confinement, unless 'B' will sign and deliver to 'A' a promissory note binding 'B' to pay certain moneys to 'A'. 'B' signs and delivers such noted. 'A' has committed extortion.

Essentials of extortion.

The following are the constituents of extortion –

1. Intentionally putting a person in fear of injury to himself or another; and
2. Dishonestly Inducement.
3. Delivery of the property.

1. Intentionally puts any person in fear of injury -

To be an offence under this section, putting a person in fear of injury intentionally is a must. The fear of injury must be such that is capable of unsettling the mind of the person threatened and cause him to part with his property. Thus, it should take away the element of freeness and voluntariness from his consent. The truth of the threat under this section is immaterial.

Fear of injury need not be of physical injury. Even creating a fear of criminal charges whether true or false not amounting to an offence against the criminal law is enough. Even threat to charge before a third person is enough.

For example,

- A's child is missing and B, who does not have A's child, threatens A that he will kill A's child unless A pay's him 1 lac Rs, will amount to extortion. Similarly, guilt or innocence of the party threatened is also immaterial.

IN WALTON'S CASE 1863,

The accused threatened to expose a clergyman, who had criminal intercourse with a woman of ill repute, unless the clergyman paid certain amount to him. He was held guilty of extortion.

NIZAMUDDIN'S CASE 1923,

A refusal by A to perform marriage and to enter it in the register unless he is paid Rs 5, was not held to be extortion.

(2) Dishonest inducement.

The second critical element of extortion is that the person who has been put to fear, must Dishonestly induces a person to deliver his property to any person.

Dishonest inducement is a part of the offence. It is sufficient that there should be wrongful loss caused to an individual but the person putting the other in fear of injury must have the intention that wrongful loss should be caused. Thus, where a person honestly believing that a thing, such as cattle or money, belongs to him, tries to get it back by some threat he is not guilty of extortion.

Dishonest inducement means that the person would not have otherwise agreed to part with his property and such parting causes him a wrongful loss. Further, the property must be delivered by the person who is threatened. Though, it is not necessary to deliver the property to the person threatening.

For example,

- If 'A' threatens 'B' to deliver property to 'C', which 'B' does, A will be guilty of extortion.

(3) Delivery of property.

The delivery of the property by the person threatened is necessary. The offence of extortion is not complete until delivery of the property by the person put in fear is done.

DULEELOODDEEN SHEIKH'S CASE 1866,

Where a person offers no resistance to the carrying off of his property on account of fear and does not himself deliver it, it was held not to be extortion but robbery.

Extortion can also happen in respect of valuable security or anything signed that can become a valuable security.

For example,

- A threatens B to sign a promissory note without the amount or date filled in. This is extortion because the note can be converted to valuable security.

IN ROMESH CHANDRA ARORA'S CASE 1960,

the accused took a photograph of a naked boy and a girl by compelling them to take off their clothes and extorted money from them by threatening to publish the photograph. He was held guilty of extortion.

IN R S NAYAK VS A R ANTULEY AND ANOTHER AIR 1986,

it was held that for extortion, fear or threat must be used. In this case, chief minister A R Antuley asked the sugar cooperatives, whose cases were pending before the govt. for consideration, to donate money and promised to look into their cases. It was held that there was no fear of injury or threat and so it was not extortion.

Section 384. Punishment for extortion. -

Whoever commits extortion shall be punished with imprisonment of either description for a term which may extend to 3 years, or with fine, or with both.

In Dhananjay v. State of Bihar,

it was held by the Supreme Court that in the absence of allegation that money was paid by informant having been put in fear of injury the offence of extortion is not committed.

In this case, distinction between theft and extortion was made clear. Extortion is carried out 'repowering will of owner, while in theft offender's intention is to take without that person's consent.

Differences between theft and extortion.

Theft (Section 378)	Extortion (Section 383)
The property is taken by the offender without consent.	The property is delivered to the offender by consent although the consent is not free.
There is no element of threat.	There is an element of threat or instillment of fear because of which the consent is given.
Only movable property is subject to theft.	Any kind of property can be subjected to extortion.
Offender takes the property himself.	Property is delivered to offender.

ROBBERY AND DACOITY

Robbery

Robbery is a severe form of either theft or extortion. In certain circumstances, a theft or an extortion gravitates to robbery. Section 390 defines robbery as follows -

Section 390 – Robbery
In all robbery there is either theft or extortion.

When theft is robbery. -

Theft is "robbery" if, in order to the committing of the theft, or in committing theft or in carrying away or attempting to carry away property obtained by theft, the offender for that end, voluntarily causes or attempts to cause to any death or hurt or wrongful restraint, or fear of instant death or of instant hurt, or of instant wrongful restraint.

When extortion is robbery. -

Extortion is "robbery" if the offender, at the time of committing the extortion, is in the presence of the person put in fear, and commits the in extortion by putting that person in fear of instant death, of instant hurt, or of instant wrongful restraint to that person, or to some other person, and by so putting in fear induces the person so put in fear then and there to deliver up the thing extorted.

Explanation. -
The offender is said to be present if he is sufficiently near to put the other person in fear of instant death, or instant hurt, or of instant wrongful restraint.

Elaboration of the Section.

Robbery by theft.

Thus, a theft becomes a robbery when the following two conditions are satisfied -

1. when someone voluntarily causes or attempts to cause
    a. death, hurt, or wrongful restraint or
    b. fear of instant death, instant hurt, or instant wrongful restraint
2. the above act is done
    a. in order to the committing of theft or
    b. committing theft or
    c. carrying away or attempting to carry away property obtained by theft.

For example,

- A holds Z down, and fraudulently takes Z's money from Z's clothes, without Z's consent. A has committed theft and in order to commit that theft, he voluntarily caused wrongful restraint to Z. Thus, A has committed robbery.

Robbery can be committed even after the theft is committed if in order to carrying away the property acquired after theft, death, hurt, or wrongful restraint or an instant fear of them is caused.

FOR THAT END. -

The expression "for that end" implies that death, hurt, or wrongful restraint or an instant fear of them is caused directly to complete the act of theft or carrying away the property.

In Hushrut Sheik's case 1866,

C and D were stealing mangoes from tree and were surprised by B. C knocked down B and B became senseless. It was held to be a case of robbery.

ACT MUST BE VOLUNTARY.

The action causing death, hurt, or wrongful restraint or an instant fear of them must be voluntary.

Edward's case 1843,

A person, while cutting a string tied to a basket accidentally cut the wrist of the owner who tried to seize it. He was held guilty of only theft.

Robbery by extortion.

An extortion becomes a robbery when the following three conditions are satisfied -

1. when a person commits extortion by putting another person in fear of instant death, hurt, or wrongful restraint, and
2. such a person induces the person put in such fear to deliver the property then and there and
3. the offender is in the presence of the person put in such fear at the time of extortion.

For example,

- A meets Z on high road, shows a pistol, and demands Z's purse. Z in consequence surrenders his purse. Here, A has extorted the purse from Z by putting him in fear of instant hurt and being present at the time of committing the extortion in his presence, A has committed robbery.

- A meets Z and Z's child on the high road. A takes the child and threatens to fling it down a precipice unless Z delivers his purse. Z in consequence, delivers the purse. Here, A has extorted the purse from Z by causing Z to be in fear of instant hurt of his child who is present there. Thus, A has committed robbery.

The violence, which is necessary to make out a robbery, must have been used for one of the purposes mentioned in Section 390. Where a man was trying to steal a basket which was tied to a cart, and the owner stretched out his arm to lay hold of it just at the moment when the thief was cutting the string with a knife and the prosecutor's wrist was cut, upon which he released his hold and the prisoner made off with basket, this was held to be only theft as the wound was a mere accident. It would have been different if it had been inflicted to make the owner give up the grasp. Similarly, where a thief finding himself to be observed, abandoned the thing stolen and ran away and while running away throws stones on the owner to avoid pursuit, the offender is not guilty of robbery.

INSTANT FEAR.

For extortion to become robbery, the fear of instant death, hurt, or wrongful restraint is must. Thus, when A obtains property from Z by saying, "Your child is with my gang and will be put to death unless you send us ten thousand rupees", this is extortion but not robbery because the person is not put in fear of instant death of his child.

IN PRESENCE OF THE PERSON -

The offender must be present where a person is put in fear of injury to commit the offence of robbery. By present, it means that the person should be sufficiently near to cause the fear. By his presence, the offender is capable of carrying out his threat immediately. Thus, the person put in such fear delivers the property in order to avoid the danger of instant death, hurt or wrongful restraint.

SHIKANDAR VS STATE 1984,

the accused attacked his victim by knife many times and succeeded in acquiring the ear rings and key from her salwar. He was held guilty of robbery.

Other cases.

In Venu alias Venugopal v. State of Karnataka,

appellants allegedly intercepted victim and robbed gold and cash by threatening with a knife. It was held that evidence of victim, her husband and recovery of vehicle used clearly established commission of offence of robbery by appellants. Offence was committed at night on public road not a highway, therefore, conviction of appellants is proper.

Smith v. Desmoud,

The essence of the offence is that violence is done or threatened to the person of the custodian; who stands between the robber and the property, in order to prevent or overcome his resistance or to oblige him to part with the property and to submit to the thief stealing it. Thus, the offence against the person and the theft are committed. Where the sequence of events is not planned, but there is an assault which happens to be followed by a theft. There must be room for niceties of argument. Where, however, the whole sequence appears to be one planned transaction, one must regard the events as a whole to see if together they amount to robbery. A thief cannot escape the charge of robbery by merely planning his crime in two stages, namely, first violently removing the owner or custodian of the property from its vicinity to a distance at which he cannot see or hear the actual stealing of the property and then, secondly, stealing the property.

Dacoity

As per section 391, a Robbery committed by five or more persons is dacoity.

Section 391 – Dacoity.

When five or more persons conjointly commit or attempt to commit robbery, or where the whole number of persons conjointly committing or attempting to commit a robbery, and persons present and aiding such commission or attempt, amount to five or more, every person so committing, attempting, or aiding is said to commit dacoity.

Conjointly implies a collective effort to commit or attempting to commit the action. It is not necessary that all the persons must be at the same place but they should be united in their efforts with respect to the offence. Thus, persons who are aiding the offence are also counted and all are guilty of dacoity.

It is necessary that all the persons involved must have common intention to commit the robbery. Thus, dacoity is different from robbery only in the respect of number of people committing it and is treated separately because it is considered to be a graver crime.

In Ram Chand's case 1932,

it was held that the resistance of the victim is not necessary. The victims, seeing a large number of offenders, did not resist and no force or threat was used but the offenders were still held guilty of dacoity.

In Ghamandi's case 1970,

it was held that less than five persons can also be convicted of dacoity if it is proved as a fact that there were more than 5 people who committed the offence by only less than five were identified.

However, if 5 persons were identified and out of them 2 were acquitted, the remaining three cannot be convicted of dacoity.

Section 391. – Punishment for dacoity.

Punishment for dacoity is life imprisonment or rigorous imprisonment which may extend to 10 years and fine. If dacoits while committing dacoity also commit murder, each of the dacoits will be punished with death or imprisonment of life or rigorous imprisonment for a term which may extend to 10 years and shall also be liable to fine.

Conjointly. –

The word "conjointly" in the section means united or concerted action of the persons participating in dacoity. If the individual acts of the persons cannot be reasonably referred to dacoity, then that person cannot be convicted for dacoity.

Example.

- P was told by the group which has consorted to commit dacoity that he should borrow a boat and during the commission of dacoity, he was asked to stay in the boat at a place some five miles away from the place of dacoity and was to wait there for them. P could not be said to have conjointly committed dacoity.

Distinction between Robbery and Dacoity

The basic distinction between robbery by extortion and robbery by theft is that in the former case, the entire menace must have preceded that act of delivery of property while it is not so in the latter case, violence may be before or after puts his hand in the pocket of B and takes out his purse. B saw it and demanded it back whereupon A threatened him with dire consequences. B went away, it was theft, not robbery. Had A said, B before putting his hand in B's pocket that if B would not handover his purse to him, he would be put to dire consequences it would have been robbery.

Section 397. – Dacoity with deadly weapon.

If at the time of committing robbery or dacoity, the offender uses any deadly weapon, or causes grievous hurt to any person, or attempts to cause death or grievous hurt to any person, the imprisonment with which such offender shall be punished shall not be less than 7 years.

Phool Kumar v. Delhi Administration,

The Supreme Court observed that where an accused, at the time of committing robbery, carries in his hand a knife opened to the view of the victims, it is sufficient to frighten or terrorise them and he can be convicted under Section 397.

Niranjan Singh v. State of Madhya Pradesh,

it was held by the Supreme Court that actual causing of grievous hurt is sufficient. In this case, accused caused knife injury on chest just below the nipple. Therefore, considering place of injury conviction of accused under Section 397, IPC was held to be proper.

Criminal MISAPPROPRIATION OF PROPERTY

Section 403. Dishonest misappropriation of property. - Whoever dishonestly misappropriated or converts to his own use any movable property, shall be punished with imprisonment of either description for a term which may extend to 2 years or with fine, or with both.

Explanation 1. - A dishonest misappropriation for a time -only is a misappropriation within the meaning of this section.

Explanation 2. -A person who finds property not in the possession of any other person, and takes such property for the purpose of protecting it for, or of restoring it to the owner, does not take or misappropriate it dishonestly, and is not guilty of an offence; but he is guilty of the offence above defined, if he appropriates it to his own use, when he knows or has the means of discovering the owner, or before he has used reasonable means to discover and give notice to the owner and has kept the property for a reasonable time to enable the owner to claim it.

What are reasonable means or what is a reasonable time in such a case, is a question of fact.

ESSENTIAL INGREDIENTS

(1) The offender initially was having possession of some movable property lawfully or without any wrong; and

(2) He dishonestly misappropriated or converts that property to his own use.

(1) Possession of Movable property. -

Only movable property can be the subject-matter of criminal misappropriation. A bull set at large in accordance with Hindu religious usage is not 'property' of any one, and not the subject of ownership by any person as the original owner has surrendered all his rights as its proprietor and has given the animal its freedom to go wherever it chose.

(2) Dishonestly misappropriated or converts to his own use. -

There must be actual conversion of the thing misappropriated to the accused's own use. Where, therefore, the accused found a thing, and merely retained it in his possession, he was acquitted of this offence.

It so happens that a person finds some property lying somewhere and picks it up with the intention of restoring it to the rightful owner. At this stage, there is no misappropriation, but later on, he changes his mind and appropriates it for his own use, even though he knows who is the owner or has means to discover the owner, or before he has used reasonable means to discover the owner or to give notice to the owner, e.g., A finds ten rupee note lying on the footpath. He picks it and keeps it. He does not know who the owner is. A has not committed the offence. On the other hand, A finds a purse containing 20-hundred-rupee currency notes. On the purse, an address of the owner is inscribed. Without caring to find out the owner, keeps the purse for his use. He is guilty of criminal misappropriation.

In Narain Singh v. State of M.P., it was held that where the accused happened to be chairman of a Samiti and he retained a certain amount of money which he had recovered from members of the Samiti and retention continued even after he ceased to be Chairman, the act of retention would not amount to criminal breach of trust, because an offence of criminal breach of trust involves entrustment which is absent in this case.

Amounts recovered from members were dues and receipts were issued to them in respect of the same act of the accused would amount to criminal misappropriation punishable under Section 403 of the Act.

Section 404. Dishonest misappropriation of property possessed by deceased person at the time of his death. Whoever dishonestly, misappropriates or converts to his own use property, knowing that such property was in the possession of a deceased person at the time of that person's disease, and has not since been in the possession of any person legally entitled to such possession, shall be punished with imprisonment of either description for a term which may extend to three years and shall also be liable to fine; and if the offender at the time of such person's disease was employed by him as a clerk or servant, the imprisonment may extend to 7 years.

This section protects the property during an interval which elapses between the time when the possessor of the property dies and the time when it comes into the possession of some person or officer authorised to take charge fit.

Distinction between criminal misappropriation and criminal breach of trust.

Distinction between criminal misappropriation and criminal breach of trust is as follows: -

1. In case of criminal breach of trust, there is conversion of property held by a person in a fiduciary capacity whereas in

case of criminal misappropriation, the possession of misappropriated property may come in any way.
2. In cause of criminal breach of trust, there is some kind of contractual relationship, either express or implied between the parties whereas in criminal misappropriation there is no such relationship.
3. In case of criminal breach of trust, the offender is lawfully entrusted with the property and he thereafter misappropriates the same or wilfully suffers any other person to do so instead of discharging the trust attached to it whereas in case of criminal misappropriation, the misappropriated property comes into the possession of the offender by any causality, such as, accidentally or otherwise and thereafter it is converted by him for the purpose of his own use.

Criminal Breach of trust.

Section 405. Criminal breach of trust. -

Whoever, being in any manner entrusted with property, or with any dominion over property, dishonestly misappropriated or converts to his own use that property, or dishonestly uses or disposes of that property in violation any direction of law prescribing the mode in which such trust is to be discharged, or of any legal contract, express or implied, which he had made touching the discharge of such trust, or wilfully suffers any other person so to do, commits "criminal breach of trust."

Explanation 1. - A person being an employer of an establishment whether exempted under Section 17 of the Employees' Provident Funds and Miscellaneous Provisions Act, 1952 or not, who deducts the employee's contribution from the wages payable to the employee for credit to a Provident Fund or Family Pension

Fund established by law for the time being in force, shall be deemed to have been entrusted with the amount of the contribution so deducted by him and if he makes default in the payment of such contribution to the said Fund in violation of the said law, shall be deemed to have dishonestly used the amount of the said contribution in violation of a direction of law as aforesaid.

Explanation 2. -A person, being an employer, who deducts the employee's contribution from the wages payable to the employees for credit to the Employees' State Insurance Fund held and administered by the Employees' State Insurance Act, 1948, shall be deemed to have been entrusted with the amount of the contribution so deducted by him and if he makes default in the payment of such contribution to the said Fund in violation of the said Act, shall be deemed to have dishonestly used the amount of the said contribution in violation of a direction of law as aforesaid.

ESSENTIAL INGREDIENTS

1. Entrusting any person with property or with any dominion over property;
2. The person entrusted -
    a. dishonestly misappropriated or converts to his own use that property, or
    b. dishonestly uses or disposes of that property or wilfully suffers any other person go to do in violation -
        i. of any direction of law prescribing the mode in which such trust is to be discharged, or
        ii. of any legal Contract made touching the discharge of such trust.

Property. -The section as such is applicable to movable property. But in some cases, it has been held to apply to immovable also, because the word 'property is used in this section without any adjective:

Trust. -The term 'trust' has been used not merely in the strict sense but in the widest possible connotation. Covering any arrangement by which one person is authorised to deal with the property for the benefit of another. Some sort of entrustment is necessary for the application of the section.

In R. V. John McIver, one S made a false representation to P that he had entered into a contract with Imperial Bank to hand over bonds worth Rs. 3,0,000 at a near date but for ratification, bonds had to be sent back to Bombay and it was not likely that he would get them back in time. He, therefore, requested P to accommodate him for about 15 days by giving bonds of that amount. P accommodated him. But S misappropriated the whole amount. The majority held that since there was no entrustment, no offence under Section 405 was committed.

The Court also distinguished in this case theft and misappropriation and observed as follows:

"In theft,' the original taking is without honesty and consent. In criminal breach of trust, the original taking is with honesty and with consent. In regard to criminal misappropriation, the original taking is honest but without the consent of the owner. In regard to the offence of cheating, the original taking is dishonest but with the consent of the owner."

In Gurumahanty Appalasamy, the accused was entrusted with a pair of earrings for the purpose or raising Rs. 7/- only upon them for the complainant's use, but he pledged them for a larger amount, gave Rs. 7/- to the complainant and applied the additional amount to his own use without telling him what he had done. He was held liable under Section 405.

In Madho Singh, the respondent's husband was a member of a housing society and he had entered into an agreement with the society whereby the society agreed to sell a plot measuring 3600 sq. ft. for Rs. 12,200. The money was paid. After the death of her husband Kamla Devi was substituted as a member of the society in place of her deceased husband. The society sold half of the plot to a third party and handed over to the complainant Kamla Devi a proposed sale deed for 1800 sq. ft. only. Kamla Devi filed a complaint under Section 405, IPC It was held that though civil remedy was available in this case but criminal court could not be prevented from taking cognizance of offence under Section 405, IPC

Aggravated form of criminal breach of trust. -in the following cases, criminal breach of trust is in an aggravated form:
(1) By a carrier, wharfinger or warehouse-keeper (S. 407);
(2) By a clerk or servant (S. 408); and
(3) By a public servant, banker, merchant, factor, broker, attorney or agent (S.409)

Jai Krishan Das v. State of Bombay, two directors of a textile mill were entrusted with certain length of cloth for dyeing under a tender. The directors delivered only half of the length of the cloth duly dyed and failed to account for the remaining. The cloth was found missing from the factory. The directors took the plea that it was eaten away by white ants. The directors were prosecuted under Section 409 and were convicted.

OF CHEATNG

Section 415. Cheating. —

Whoever, by deceiving any person, fraudulently or dishonestly induces the person so deceived to deliver any property to any person, or to consent that any person shall retain any property, or intentionally induces the person.so deceived to do or omit to do anything which he would not do or omit if he were not so deceived, and which act or omission causes or is likely to cause damage or harm to that person in body, reputation or property, is said to "cheat".

Explanation. - A dishonest concealment of facts is a deception within the meaning of this session.

ESSENTIAL INGREDIENTS

(1) Deception of any person;
(2)
    (a) Fraudulently or dishonestly inducing that person –
        (1) to deliver any property to any person, or
        (2) to consent that any person shall retain property, or
    (b) Intentionally inducing that person to do or omit to do anything which he would not do or omit if he were not so deceived, and which act or omission causes or is likely to cause damage or harm to that person in body, mind, reputation or property.

(1) Deceiving any person. –

Whenever a person fraudulently represents something as an existing fact which is actually not an existing fact, he commits this offence. A of a definite fact with intent to defraud, cognizable by the senses - as where a seller represents the quantity of coal to be fourteen cwt., whereas- it is in fact only eight cwt. but so packed as to look more, or where the seller, by manoeuvring, to pass off fastens of cheese as if extracted from the cheese offered for sale, what-was it is not - is a cheating.

(2) Fraudulent or dishonest inducement to deliver property. –

The essence of the charge under Section 415 is that the accused induces someone fraudulently or dishonestly. A representation must have been made knowing it to be false resulting in wrongful loss or wrongful gain.2 A and B in concert entice away a boy below 15 years in order to murder him The boy is actually murdered. A and B anonymously demanded a ransom from F, the father of the deceased boy on the pretext that the boy would return if the ransom was paid. The ransom is paid but the boy was not recovered. Here, A and B would be liable for murder of the boy as well as for cheating because they had induced F with dishonest intention to pay the ransom.

(3) Or to consent that any person shall retain any property. –

It is cheating whether a deception causes a person fraudulently or dishonestly to acquire property by delivery, or to retain property already in his possession.

(4) Intentionally inducing that person to do or omit to do anything which he would not do or omit, etc. –

The person cheated must have been intentionally induced to do an act which he would not have done or to omit to do an act which he would have done. Owing to the deception practiced on him. Intention, therefore, is the gist of offence of
cheating. To hold a person guilty of cheating it is necessary to show that he had fraudulent or dishonest intention at the time of making the promise. It has been held in Ramautar choukhany case that deception is of the essence of the offence of cheating.

Mere failure to honour a promise does not by itself constitute the offence of cheating.

(5) Which act or omission causes or is likely to cause damage or harm in body, mind, reputation or property. –

It is necessary that the harm should be caused to the person deceived. Damage or harm in mind covers both, injury to mental faculties or mental pain or anguish, Where the accused falsely identified a person before the Oath Commissioner and thus, induced him to attest an affidavit, it was held that no offence under Section 419, IPC was committed as the Oath Commissioner did not suffer any harm in body, mind, reputation or property.

The explanation added to the section refers to the actual deception itself and not to the concealment of a deception by someone else. For the purpose of this section the concealment of fact need not be illegal if it is dishonest.

In Martindale, the accused presented a cheque, in part payment of goods purchased, to A, a shop salesman, who sent for R, and there was a conversation between them in a language which the accused did not understand, and R thereupon cashed the cheque and the amount, less the discount and the price of the goods, was paid to the accused. It was held that the offence of cheating R was established, as the tender of the cheque as a genuine one carried with it the representation to R, through A, that it would be honoured on presentation, and that the omission to disclose to A, the fact that he had no money in the bank to meet the cheque, and that it would be dishonoured on presentation was a dishonest concealment under this explanation.

Section 416. Cheating by personation. -

A person is said to "cheat by personation" if he cheats by pretending to be some other person, or by knowingly substituting one person for another, representing that he or any other person is a person other than he or such person really is.

Explanation. -The offence is committed whether the individual personated is real or imaginary person.

ESSENTIAL INGREDIENTS

(1) Pretension by a person to be some other person;
(2) Knowingly substituting one person for another; and
(3) Representation that he or any other person is a person other than he or such person really is.

IN ASHWINI KUMAR GUPTA,

A falsely represented himself to B at a University Examination, got a hall ticket under B's name, and wrote papers in B's name, it was held that A was guilty of cheating by personation and forgery.

Section 419. Punishment.

Punishment for cheating by cheating by personation shall be punished with imprisonment of either description for a term which may extend to 3 years, or with fine, or with both.

Section 420. Cheating and dishonestly inducing delivery of property. -

Whoever cheats and thereby dishonestly induces the person deceived to deliver any
property to any person, or to make, alter or destroy the whole or any part of a valuable security, or anything which is signed or sealed, and which is capable of being converted into a valuable security, shall be punished with imprisonment of either

description for a term which may extend to 7 years, and shall also be liable to fine.

SOUBHANA COKE PRODUCTS V. STATE OF U.P.,

It was held that the offence of cheating can be made out only if it has been shown that damage or harm has been caused to the person so deceived.

THOMAS VARGISH V. P. JEROME,

A cheque was returned unpaid by the bank under the remark "payment stopped by drawer". The complainant alleged that the cheque was dishonoured because the drawer of the cheque had no sufficient balance or arrangement'. The Court refused to quash the complaint. Issuing a cheque without arrangement of sufficient funds may amount to cheating.

N. DEVENDRAPPA V. STATE OF KARNATAKA,

Accused had induced complainant and many others from parting with their money as part payment for sale of land not owned by him. Bogus receipts were also issued. It was held that under the circumstances dishonest of accused is proved and his conviction under Section 420, IPC is proper.

MISCHIEF

Section 425. Mischief. -

Whoever, with intent to cause, or knowing that he is likely to cause, wrongful loss or damage to the public or to any person, causes the destruction of any property, or any such change in any property or in the situation thereof as destroys or diminishes its value or utility, or affects it injuriously, commits "mischief'.

Explanation 1.

It is not essential to the offence of mischief that the offender should intend to cause loss or damage to the owner of the property injured or destroyed. It IS sufficient if he intends to cause, or knows that he is likely to cause, wrongful loss or damage to any person by injuring any property, whether it belongs to that person or not.

Explanation 2.

Mischief may be committed by an act affecting property belonging to the person who commits the act, or to that person and others jointly.

Section 426. Punishment for mischief. -

Whoever commits mischief shall be punished with imprisonment of either description for a term which may extend to 3 months, or with fine, or with both.

ESSENTIAL INGREDIENTS.

(1) Intention or knowledge of likelihood to cause wrongful loss or damage to the public or to any person;
(2) Causing the destruction of some property or any change in it or in its situation and
(3) Such change must destroy or diminish its value or utility, or affects it injuriously.

In Abdul Hussain,

A had a dispute about the possession of certain land with C. C dug a well with a view to cultivate the said land, but forcibly entered on the land and damaged the well. A would be guilty of mischief even though C was a trespasser.

In Ram Krishna Singh, if a person sets fire to his own house in order to eject a trespasser, he cannot be said to cause wrongful loss to any person or the public and will not be liable for the offence of mischief.

CRMINAL TRESPASS

Section 441. Criminal trespass. -

Whoever enters into or upon property in the possession of another with intent to commit an offence or to intimidate, insult or annoy any person in possession of such property or having lawfully entered into or upon such property, unlawfully remains there with intent thereby to intimidate, insult or annoy any such person, or with intent to commit an offence, is said to commit "criminal trespass".

ESSENTIAL INGREDIENTS

(1) Entry into or upon property in the possession of another;
(2) If such entry is lawful, then unlawfully remaining upon such property.
(3) Such entry or unlawfully remaining must be with intent –
    (a) to commit an offence; or
    (b) to intimidate insult or annoy any person in possession of the property.

(1) Entry into or upon property in the possession of another

'Property in the section means immovable corporeal property. The possession over the property must be actual possession of some person other than the alleged trespasser. The offence can only be committed against a person who is in actual physical possession of the property in question. If the complainant is not in actual possession of the property this offence cannot be committed.

GHASI CASE,

A man may be guilty of criminal trespass on the land of another without ever personally setting foot on it if, e.g., he causes others to build on it against the wishes and in spite of the protest of its owner.

PONNUSAMY V. MAHIPATHI,

Where a person who unlawfully entered into or upon the property in the possession of another was held guilty of the offence of criminal trespass under this section, he could not again be prosecuted for an offence under the section; if he unlawfully continued to remain there with one of the intentions mentioned in the section. The offence was complete as soon as there was unlawful entry, and he could not be prosecuted again for remaining there as he had already been convicted under this section.

(2) Intent to commit an offence.

Criminal trespass depends on the intention of the offender and not upon the nature of the act, e.g., a person with intent to save his family and property from imminent destruction commits civil trespass on his neighbour's land, and cuts a portion of a dam belonging to his neighbour, he is not guilty of criminal trespass.

(3) Or to intimidate, insult or annoy any person in possession. -

Trespass is an offence only if it is committed with one of the intents specified in the section. In order to establish that the entry on the property was with intent to annoy, intimidate or insult it is necessary for the Court to be satisfied that causing such annoyance intimidation or insult was the main aim of the entry.

(4) Having lawfully entered into or upon such property, unlawfully remains there. -

The original entry of a person may be lawful on the premises of another but if he remains on the property with the aforesaid intent, he commits trespass. A and B, the two rival claimants to some immovable property, including a certain shop, A was in possession of the shop through a tenant. The tenant, however, vacated the shop, whereupon B occupied and locked it up. It was held that A could not, at the time of the occurrence, be said to be in possession of the shop within the meaning of this section and that the intention of B was not necessarily required to constitute the offence of criminal trespass within the meaning of this section.

Section 442. House-trespass. -

Whoever commits criminal trespass by entering into or remaining in any building, tent or vessel used as a human dwelling or any building used as a place for worship, or as a place for the custody of property, is said to commit "house trespass".

Explanation. - The introduction of any part of the criminal trespasser's body is entering sufficient to constitute house trespass.

Section 443. Lurking house-trespass. -

Whoever commits house-trespass having taken precautions to conceal such house-trespass from some person who has a right to exclude or eject the trespasser from the building, tent or vessel which is the subject of trespass, is said to commit "lurking house-trespass".

Section 444. Lurking house-trespass by night. -

Whoever commits lurking house-trespass after sunset and before sunrise, is said to commit "lurking house-trespass by night."

Section 445. Housebreaking. -

A person is said to commit "housebreaking" WHO commits house-trespass if he affects his entrance into the house or any part of it in any of the 6 ways hereinafter described; or if, being in the house or any part of it for the purpose of committing an offence, or, having committed an offence therein, he quits the house or any part of it in any of such 6 ways, that is to say: -

(1) If he enters or quits through a passage made by himself or by any, abettor of the house-trespass, in order to the committing of the house-trespass;

(2) If he enters or quits through any passage not intended by any person, other than himself or an abettor of the offence, for human entrance, or through any passage which he has obtained access by scaling or climbing over any wall or building;

(3) If he enters or quits through any passage which he or any abettor of the house-trespass has opened, in order to the committing of the house-trespass by any means by which that passage was not intended by the occupier of the house to be opened;

(4) If he enters or quits by opening any lock in order to the committing of the house-trespass or in order to the quitting of the house after a house-trespass;

(5) If he affects his entrance or departure by using criminal force or committing an assault, or by threatening any person with assault; and

(6) If he enters or quits through any passage which he knows to have been fasten against such entrance or departure, and to have been unfastened by himself or by an abettor of the house-trespass.

Explanation. -

Any outhouse or building occupied with a house and such house there is an immediate internal communication, is part of the house within the meaning of this section.

House trespass may be aggravated by being committed in a violent manner. The one type is lurking house-trespass, and another is house breaking. The intent necessary to prove 'criminal trespass' must be present and the court must come to a definite inference as to the intention with which the entry was affected. Lurking house-trespass or housebreaking by night is punishable under Section 456, IPC

CHAPTER 18 - OF OFFENCES RELATING TO DOCUMENTS AND TO PROPERTY MARKS [463 TO 489]

Section 463. Forgery. -

Whoever makes any false document or false electronic record or part of a document or electronic record with intent to cause damage or injury, to the public or to any person, or to support any claim or title, or to cause any person to part with property, or to enter into any express or implied contract, or with intent to commit fraud or that fraud may be committed, commits forgery.

Section 464. -Making a false document. -

A person is said to make a false document or false electronic record, -

First. -Who dishonestly or fraudulently -

(a) makes, signs, seals or executes a document or part of a document;

(b) makes or transmits any electronic record or part of any electronic record;

(c) affixes any [electronic signature] on any electronic record;

(d) makes any mark denoting the execution of a document or the authenticity of the [electronic signature];

With the intention of causing, it to be believed that such document or part of document, electronic record or [electronic signature] was made, signed, sealed, executed, transmitted or affixed by or by the authority of a person by whom or by whose authority he knows that it was not made, signed, sealed, executed or affixed; or

Secondly. -who, without lawful authority, dishonestly, or fraudulently, by cancellation or otherwise, alters a document or an electronic record in any material part thereof, after it has been made, executed or affixed with electronic signature either by himself or by any other person, whether such person be living or dead at the time of such alteration; or

Thirdly. -who dishonestly or fraudulently causes any person to 8ign, seal, execute or alter a document or an electronic record or to affix his [electronic signature] on any electronic record knowing that such person by reason of unsoundness of mind or intoxication cannot, or that by reason of deception practised upon him, he does not know the contents of the document or electronic record or the nature of the alteration.

Illustrations

(a) A has a letter of credit upon B for rupees 10,000 written by Z, A in order to defraud B, adds a cipher to the 10,000 and makes the sum intending that it may be believed by B that Z so wrote the letter. A has committed forgery.

(b) A, without Z's authority, affixed Z's seal to a document purporting to be a conveyance of an estate from Z to A, with the intention of selling the estate to B and thereby of obtaining from B the purchase money. A has committed forgery.

(c) A pick up a cheque on a banker signed by B, payable to bearer, but without any sum having been inserted in the cheque. A fraudulently fills up the cheque by inserting the sum of ten thousand rupees. A commits forgery.

(d) A leaf with B, his agent, a cheque on a banker, signed by A, without inserting the sum payable and authorizes B to fill up the cheque by inserting a sum not exceeding ten thousand rupees for the purpose of making certain payments. B fraudulently fills up the cheque by inserting the sum of twenty thousand rupees. B commits forgery.

(e) A draws a bill of exchange on himself in the name of B without B's authority intending to discount it as a genuine bill with a banker and intending to take up the bill on its maturity. Here, as A draws the bill with intent to deceive the banker by leading him to suppose that he had the security of B, and thereby to discount the bill, A is guilty of forgery.

(f) Z's will contain these words. - "I direct that all my remaining property be equally divided between A, B, and C." A dishonestly scratches out B's name, intending that it may be believed that the whole was left to himself, and C. A has committed forgery.

(g) A endorses a Government promissory note and makes it payable to Z or his order by writing on the bill the words "Pay to Z or his order" and signing the endorsement. B dishonestly erases the words "Pay to Z or his order" and thereby converts the special endorsement into a blank endorsement. B commits forgery.

(h) A sell and conveys an estate to Z. A, afterwards, in order to defraud Z of his estate, executes a conveyance of the same estate to B, dated six months earlier than the date of conveyance to Z, intending it to be believed that he had conveyed the estate to B before he conveyed It to Z. A has committed forgery.

(i) Z dictates his will to A. An intentionally writes down a different legatee from the legatee named by Z, and by representing to Z that he has prepared the will according to his instructions, induces Z to sign the will. A has committed forgery.

(j) A write a letter and signs it with B'3 name without B's authority, certifying that A is a man of good character and in distressed circumstances from unforeseen misfortune, intending by means of such letter to obtain alms from Z and other persons. Here, as A made a false document in order to induce Z to part with property, A has committed forgery.

(k) A without B's authority writes a letter and signs it in B's name certifying to A's character, intending thereby to obtain employment under Z. A has committed forgery inasmuch as he intended to deceive Z by the forged certificate and thereby to induce Z to enter into an express or implied contract for service.

Explanation 1.

A man's signature of his own name may amount to forgery.

Illustrations

(a) A sign his own name to a bill of exchange intending that it may be believed that the bill was drawn by another person of the same name. A has committed forgery.

(b) A write the words "accepted" on a piece of paper and signs it with Z's name, in order that B may afterwards write on the paper a bill of exchange drawn by B upon Z, and negotiate the bill as though it has been accepted by Z. A is guilty of forgery; and if B, Showing the fact, draws the bill upon the paper pursuant to A's intention, B is also guilty of forgery.

(c) A pick up a bill of exchange payable to the order of a different person with the same name endorses the bill in his own name, intending to cause it to be believed that it was endorsed by the person to whose order it was payable; here A has committed forgery.

(d) A purchase an estate sold under execution of a decree against B. B, after the seizure of the estate in collusion with Z, executes a lease of the estate to Z at a nominal rent for a long period and dates the lease six months prior to the seizure, with intent to defraud A, and to cause it to be believed that the lease was granted before the seizure. B, though he executes the lease in his own name, commits forgery by antedating it.

(e) A. a trader, in anticipation of insolvency, lodges effects with B for A's benefit, and with intent to defraud his creditors; and in order to give a colour to the transaction writes a promissory note binding himself to pay B a sum for value received, and antedates the note, intending that it may be believed to have been made before A was on the point of insolvency. A has committed forgery under the first head of the definition.

Explanation 2. -The making of a false document in the name of a fictitious person, intending it to be believed that the document was made by a real person, or in the name of a deceased person, intending it to be believed that the document was made by the person in his lifetime, may amount to forgery.

Illustration

A draws a bill of exchange upon a fictitious person, and fraudulently accepts the bill in the name of such fictitious person with intent to negotiate it. A commits forgery.

Explanation 3. -For the purposes of this section the expression "affixing [electronic si31ature]" shall have the meaning assigned to it in. clause (d) of sub-section (1) of section 2 of the Information Technology Act, 2000.

Section 465. Punishment for forgery. -

Whoever commits forgery shall be punished with imprisonment of either description for a term which may extend to 2 years, or with fine, or with both.

INGREDIENTS OF FORGERY

(1) The making of a false document or part of it;
(2) Such making should be with intent -
 (a) to cause damage or injury to the public or any person, or
 (b) to support any claim or title, or
 (c) to cause any person to part with property, or
 (d) to cause any person to enter into an express or implied contract, or
 (e) to commit fraud or that fraud may be committed.

The offence of forgery is complete if a document, false in fact, is made with intent to commit a fraud, although it may not have been made with any one of the other intents specified in Section 463. In other words, to constitute forgery apart from making of a false document; it is very necessary to show that there was defrauding also i.e., deceit and injury. In Sadanand, the accused had signed the power of attorney representing himself as one R and had filed the same before S.T.A. to support the complaint made in the name of R regarding the conduct of official business by the Directorate of Transport, it was held that he had not committed the offence of forgery under Section 466 or using a forged document as genuine under Section 471, IPC, as there was no attempt to deceive anybody and to gain some advantage or cause injury to another.

Muhammad Saeed Khan case.

It has been held that where there is an intention to deceive and by means of the deceit to obtain an advantage, there is fraud, and if a document is fabricated with such intent it is a forgery.

A general intention to defraud, without the intention of causing wrongful gain to one person or wrongful loss to another will be sufficient to support a conviction. In Dr. Vimla case, the Supreme Court has held that the expression "defraud" involves two elements, namely, deceit and injury to the person deceived. Injury is something other than economic loss, that is, deprivation of property whether movable or immovable, or of money, and it will include harm whatever caused to any person in body, mind, reputation or such others. It is a non-economic or non-pecuniary loss. A benefit or advantage to the deceiver will almost always cause loss or detriment to the deceived. Even in those cases where there is a benefit or advantage to the deceiver but no corresponding loss to the deceived the latter condition that is, injury is satisfied.

Further, to constitute the offence of forgery the document must be made dishonestly and fraudulently, e.g., where A removes from the file of the Court a written statement filed by him and substitutes another Writing as if to show that the latter writing was the one which was originally filed, it amounts to making of a false document fraudulently and dishonestly.

The second clause of the section requires dishonest or fraudulent cancellation or alteration of a document in any material part without lawful authority after it has been made or executed by a person who may be living or dead.

The third clause deals with cases where the person making the document is not supposed to know its contents owing to unsoundness of mind or intoxication or deception.

Explanation (1) makes it clear that there may be sufficient falsity where a man only signs his own name if he does so in order that it may be mistaken for the signature of another person of the same name. If a cheque payable to B or order gets into the hands of A no -is person of the same name as the payee and A knowing that he was not the real person in 'n hose favour it was drawn, endorses it, he would be guilty of forgery.

Explanation (2) makes it clear that a document will be forgery if it is a false document even in the name of a fictitious person. To support a charge of forgery it is immaterial whether the name forged is that of a fictitious person '. who never existed or of a real person. Section 466. Forgery of record of Court or of Public register etc. -

Whoever forges a

document or an electronic record, purporting to be a record or proceeding of or in a Court of Justice, or a register of birth, baptism, marriage or burial or a register kept by a public servant as such, or a certificate or a document purporting to be made by a public servant in his official

capacity, or an authority to institute or defend a suit, or to take any proceedings therein, or to confess judgment, or a power of attorney, shall be punished with imprisonment of - either description for a term which may extend to seven years, and shall also be liable to fine.

Explanation. -For the purposes of this section, register includes any list data or record of any entries maintained in the electronic form as defined in clause (r) of sub-section (1) of Section 2 of the Information Technology Act, 2000.

This section applies to cases where a certificate or a document is forged by a person with a view to make it appear that it was duly issued by a public office, e.g., forging a marriage certificate.

Section 467. Forgery of valuable security, will, etc. -

Whoever, forges a document which purports to be valuable security, or a will, or an authority to adopt a son or, which purports to give authority to any person to make or transfer any valuable security, or to receive the principal, interest or dividends thereon, or to receive or deliver any money, movable property, or valuable security, or any document purporting to be an acquittance or receipt acknowledging the payment of money, or an acquittance or receipt for the delivery of any movable property or valuable security, shall be punished with imprisonment for life, or with imprisonment of either description for a term which may extend to 10 years, and shall also be liable to fine.

The offence under Section 467 is an aggravated form of the offence described in previous section. The forged document must be one of those mentioned in the section.

Section 468. Forgery for purpose of cheating. -

Whoever commits forgery intending that the document forged shall be used for the purpose of cheating shall be punished with imprisonment of either description for a term which may extend to 7 years, and shall also be liable to fine.

In **Appasami,** A falsely represented himself to B at a University Examination, got-a hall ticket under B's name and headed and signed answer papers to questions with B's name. It was held that A was guilty of forgery and cheating by personation.

Section 469 Forgery for purpose of harming reputation. –

Whoever commits forgery, intending that the document or electronic record forged shall harm the reputation of any party, or knowing that it is likely to be used for that purpose, shall be punished with imprisonment of either description for a term which may extend to three years, and shall also be liable to fine.

Section 470. Forged document -

A false document or electronic record made wholly or in part by forgery is designated "forged document or electronic record".

Section 471. Using as genuine a forged document. -

Whoever fraudulently or dishonestly uses as genuine any document or electronic record which he knows or has reason to believe to be a forged document or electronic record, shall be punished in the same manner as if he had forged such document or electronic record.

ESSENTIAL INGREDIENTS
(1) Fraudulent or dishonest use of a document as genuine; and
(2) The person using it must have knowledge or reason to believe that the document is a forged one.

The use of a forged document under Sections 470 and 471 will be fraudulent and dishonest even though the document itself is unnecessary for the case of the party who uses it, and though, in fact, he had a perfectly good title without it the presentation of a forged document for registration and obtaining registration, is using of that document.

Abdul Ghafur,
the accused in order that he might obtain the annulment of an order adjudicating him insolvent, and that thereafter he might be in a position to tender for municipal contracts, produced before the receiver in insolvency a document which purported to be a receipt from a creditor for payment of debt which the creditor had in fact written off as irrecoverable. It was held that in respect of the use of that receipt he was guilty under Section 465 read with this section.

Mulai Singh,
the use of certified copies of forged originals by a person who knows that the originals are forged amounts to making use of forged documents within the meaning of this section.

M.M. Trivedi v. State of M.P.,

the mere fact that the document was forged would not conclude the matter for a conviction under this section. It must be established that the accused was a party to the forgery.

Section 477A: Ratification of accounts. –

Whoever, being a clerk, officer or servant, or employed or acting in the capacity of a clerk, officer or servant, wilfully, and with intent to defraud, destroys, alters, mutilates or falsifies, any book, electronic record, paper, writing, valuable security or account which belongs to or is in the possession of his employer, or has been received by him for or on behalf of his employers, or wilfully and with intent to defraud, makes or abets the making of any false entry in, or omits or alters or abets the omission or alteration of any material particular from or in, any such book, electronic record, paper, writing, valuable security or accounts, shall be punished with imprisonment of either description for a term which may extend to seven years, or with fine, or with both.

Explanation. –

It shall be sufficient in any charge under this section to allege a general intent to defraud without naming any particular person intended to be defrauded or specifying any particular sum of money intended to be the subject of fraud, or any particular day on which the offence was committed.

ESSENTIAL INGREDIENTS

(1) The person coming within its purview must be a clerk, an officer, or a servant, or he might be working as a clerk, or an officer, or a servant;

(2) He must wilfully and with intention to commit fraud -

(1) destroy, alter, or falsify any book, paper, writing or valuable security, which –

(a) belongs to his employer or is in his possession; or

(b) it has been obtained by him for or on behalf of his employer,

(2) makes or abets the making of any false entry in or omits or alters or abets the omission or alteration of any material particular from or in any such book, paper, writing, valuable security or account.

The section deals with falsification of accounts. Removal of new court fee stamps from documents and substitution in their place old and used stamps with alterations of the figures on them not fall within the scope of this section.

In **Sukhamoy Maitra,** where the accused falsified a measurement book of repairs to buildings and a bill with intent that a contractor's bill for the repairs done might be passed without actual measurement, it was held that the act of the accused amounted to a fraudulent falsification of accounts.

CHAPTER 19. OF THE CRIMINAL BREACH OF CONTRACTS OF SERVICE (490 TO 492)

CHAPTER 20 - OF OFFENCES RELATING TO MARRIAGE [493 TO 498]

Section 493. Cohabitation caused by a man deceitfully inducing a belief of lawful marriage. Every man who by deceit causes any woman who is not lawfully married to him to believe that she is lawfully married to him and to cohabit or have sexual intercourse with him in that belief, shall be punished with imprisonment of either description for a term which may extend to 10 years; and shall also be liable to fine.

ESSENTIAL INGREDIENTS

(1) Deceit causing a false belief in the existence of a lawful marriage; and

(2) Cohabitation or sexual intercourse with the person causing such belief.

Section 494. Marrying again during the lifetime of husband or wife. –

Whoever, having a husband or wife living, marries in any case in which such marriage is void by reason of it's taking place during the life of such husband or wife, shall be punished with imprisonment of either description for a term which may extend to 7 years, and shall also be liable to fine.

Exception. -This section does not intend to any person whose marriage with such husband or wife has been declared void by a Court of competent jurisdiction, nor to any person who contracts a marriage during the life of a former husband or wife, if such husband or wife, at the time of the subsequent marriage, shall have been continually absent from such person for the space of seven years, and shall not have been heard of by such person as being alive within that time, provided the person contracting such subsequent marriage shall, before such marriage takes place, inform the person with whom such marriage is contracted of the real state of facts so far as the same are within his her Knowledge.

ESSENTIAL INGREDIENTS

(1) Existence of the first wife or husband when the second marriage is celebrated; and

(2) The second marriage being void by reason of the subsistence of the first according to the law applicable to the person violating the provisions of the section.

Section 494 does not apply to Mohammedan males, who are allowed to marry more than one wife, but it applies to Mohammedan females, and to Hindus, Christians and Parsis of either sex.

(1) Existence of a valid marriage. -

There must be at the time of the second marriage a previous valid and subsisting marriage. If the first marriage is not a valid marriage no offence is committed by contracting a second marriage, e.g., if A marries B, a person within prohibited degrees of affinity and during B's lifetime marries C, A does not.

In Santosh Kumari v. Surjit Singh, divorce dissolves a valid marriage and the parties obtaining such dissolution can remarry.

In Abdul Ghani v. Azizul Haq, a Mohammedan woman marrying within the period of iddat is not guilty of bigamy.

(2) The accused marries another person, -

The word "marries" used in this section means "marries by some form of marriage known to and recognised by the law". The section comes into operation when the accused having been married once and marriage still subsisting has gone through marriage second time. The word "marry" in Section 494 means going through a form of marriage whether it be legal and valid or illegal and invalid.

The Supreme Court in Bhaurao, observed that prima facie, the expression "whoever marries" must mean "whoever marries validly" or whoever.... marries and whose marriage is a valid one. If the marriage is not a valid one according to the law applicable to the parties no question of its being void by reason of its taking place during the life of the wife or the husband of the person arises. If a marriage is not a valid marriage, it is no marriage in the eyes of claw.

In Gnanasoundari v. Nallathambi,

In a case of bigamy, the court came to the conclusion that the second marriage was invalid as one of the two essential ceremonies of the customary marriage was not performed and it was held that having so concluded the court could not proceed to convict the accused under Section 494.

In Santosh Kumari v. Surjit Singh, it was held that no Court is authorised to permit a second marriage even if it be at the application of the first wife. Such permission is illegal.

EXCEPTIONS

(1) If the second marriage takes place within 7 years under a bona fide belief based on reasonable grounds that the former concert is dead, no offence is committed.

In Thomas Jones, where the accused's first wife had left him for 16 years, and it was proved by the second wife that she had known him for 9 years, living as a single man and that she had never heard of the first wife, who it appeared, had been living 17 miles away from where the accused resided, it was held that the accused was not guilty of bigamy.

(2) Where it is proved that the accused. and his first wife have lived apart for 7 years preceding the second marriage, it is incumbent on the prosecution to show that during that time he was aware of her existence, and, in the absence of such proof, the accused is entitled to be acquitted. But a woman who, having

the means of acquiring knowledge of the fact, of the death of her first husband does not choose to make use of them, is guilty of bigamy,

(3) If the second marriage is contracted within 7 years, it is incumbent on the person contracting it to inform the other party about the first marriage. If the above facts are established by the accused, he or she shall be protected from the offence of bigamy.

Section 495. -Same offence with concealment of former marriage from person with whom subsequent marriage is contracted. Whoever commits the offence defined in the last preceding section having concealed from the person with whom the Subsequent marriage is contracted, the fact of the former marriage, shall be punished with imprisonment of either description for a term which may extend to 10 years and shall also be liable to fine.

This is an aggravated form of offence defined in Section 494.

Section 496. Marriage ceremony fraudulently gone through without lawful marriage. -

Whoever, dishonestly or with a fraudulent intention, goes through the ceremony of being married, knowing that he is not thereby lawfully married, shall be punished with imprisonment of either description for a term which may extend to 7 years and shall also be liable to fine.

ESSENTIAL INGREDIENTS

(1) Dishonestly or with fraudulent intention going through the ceremony of marriage.

(2) Knowledge on the part of the person going through the ceremony that he is not thereby lawfully married.

This section is applicable to cases in which marriage ceremony is complete but in no circumstances constitute a valid marriage and in which one of the parties is induced to believe that a valid marriage has been constituted thereby.

In Kailash Singh, where the accused married for the second time during the pendency of special appeal against the decree of divorce in violation of Section 15 of the Hindu Marriage Act but without concealing the fact of pendency of the appeal from the girl or her parents, no conviction could be entered under Section 496, IPC, as the act of the accused has neither dishonest or fraudulent.

Section 497: Adultery. —

Whoever has sexual intercourse with a person who is and whom he knows or has reason to believe to be the wife of another man, without the consent or convenience of that man, such sexual intercourse not amounting to the offence of rape, is guilty of the offence of adultery, and shall be punished with imprisonment of either description for a term which may extend to 5 years, or with fine, or with both. In such a case the wife shall not be punishable as an abettor.

ESSENTIAL INGREDIENTS

(1) Sexual intercourse by a man with a woman who is or whom he has reason to believe to be the wife of another man;

(2) Such sexual intercourse must be without the consent or connivance of the husband;

(3) Such sexual intercourse must not amount to rape.

The constitutional validity of Section 497 has been upheld by the Supreme Court in Sowmithri Vishnu v. Union of India. The

Apex Court observed that Section 497 does not envisage prosecution of the wife by the husband for adultery. Indeed, the section provides expressly that the wife shall not be punishable as an abettor. No grievance can be made that the section does not allow the wife to prosecute the husband for adultery. The contemplation of the law evidently is that the wife, who is involved in an illicit relationship with another man is a victim and not the author of the crime. The offence of adultery as defined in Section 497, is considered by the Legislature as an offence against the sanctity of the matrimonial home, an act which is committed by a man, as it generally is. Therefore, those men who define that sanctity are brought within the net of law.....The Legislature may enlarge the definition of 'adultery to keep pace with the moving times.

But, until then the law must remain as it is. The law, as it is, does not offend either Article 14 or Article 15 of the Constitution.

Complaint by the person aggrieved. -For prosecution under Section 497, complaint by the person aggrieved is necessary. No Court shall have cognizance of an offence under this section except upon a complaint made by the husband of the woman or, in his absence, made with the leave of the Court by some person who had care of such woman on his behalf at the time when such offence was committed.

Section 498: Enticing or taking away or detaining with criminal intent a married woman. –

Whoever takes or entices away any woman who is and whom he knows or has reason to believe to be the wife of any other man, from that man, or from any person having the care of her on behalf of that man, with intent that she may have illicit intercourse with any person, or conceals or detains with that intent any such woman shall be punished with imprisonment of either description for a term which may extend to 2 years, or with fine, or with both.

ESSENTIAL INGREDIENTS

(1) Taking or enticing away or concealing or detaining the wife of another man from any person having the care of her on behalf of that man;

(2) Such taking, enticing, concealing or detaining must be with intent that she may have illicit intercourse with any person; and

(3) Knowledge or reason to believe that the woman is the wife of another man.

The offence punishable under Section 498 is a minor offence as compared with an offence punishable under Section 366.

In order to satisfy a charge under this section it is necessary that the accused could be said to have detained the woman and to have detained her with intent that she may have illicit intercourse with him. The Allahabad High Court has taken the view that sexual intercourse between the woman and any person or other person than the person to whom she had been given in marriage during the life of her husband would be within the meaning of this section.

CHAPTER 20A - OF CRUELTY BY HUSBAND OR RELATIVES OF HUSBAND [498A]

Section 498A. - CRUELTY BY HUSBAND OR RELATIVES OF HUSBAND.

Whoever, being the husband or the relative of the husband of a woman, subjects such Women to cruelty shall be punished with imprisonment for a term which may extend to 3 years and shall also be liable to fine.

Explanation. - For the purpose of this section, "cruelty" means -

(a) any wilful conduct which is of such a nature as is likely to drive the Woman to commit suicide or to cause grave injury or danger to life, limb or health (whether mental or physical) of the woman; or

(b) harassment of the woman where such harassment is with a view -to coercing her or any person related to her to meet any unlawful demand for any property or valuable security or is on account of failure by her or any person related to her to meet such demand.

This section has been introduced in the Code by the Criminal Law (Amendment) Act, 1983. It is meant to meet the cases of dowry deaths. While upholding the constitutional validity of Section 498-A Supreme Court held in Krishen Lal v. Union of India, that the husband and the relatives of the husband of a married woman form a class apart by themselves and it amounts to reasonable classification especially when a married woman is treated with cruelty within the four walls of the house of her husband and there is no likelihood of any evidence available. Consequently, this section cannot be said to be violative of Article 14 of the Constitution.

Sarujakshan v. State of Maharashtra,

The wife coming from respectable orthodox family was subjected by her husband, who was of highly suspicious nature, to humiliation by demanding degrading and insulting her, calling her a prostitute, denying her family life and comfort and not permitting anybody to meet her, all this was held to be sufficient to justify the husband's conviction under Section 498-A.

Punishment of husband. -

it will be clear from the language of section 498-A, Indian Penal Code, that if a husband subjects his wife to cruelty, he shall be punished with imprisonment for a term which may extend to three years and shall also be liable to fine. The Explanation under Section 498-A defines "cruelty" for the purpose of section 498-A to mean any of the acts mentioned in Clause (a) or Clause (b). In this case Clause (b) is not attracted as there was no harassment by the husband with a view to forcing her to meet any unlawful demand for any property or valuable security or on account of failure by her to meet such demand. The first limb of Clause (a) of the Explanation of Section 498-A, Indian Penal Code, states that "cruelty" means any wilful conduct which is of such nature as is likely to drive the woman to commit suicide.

In Sarla Prabhakar Waghmare v. State of Maharashtra,

it was held that it is not every harassment or every type of cruelty that would attract Section 498-A. The complainant has conclusively to establish that the beating and harassment in question was with a view to force her to commit suicide or to fulfil the illegal demand of dowry.

In Tapan Pal v. State of W.B.,

the deceased was asked to part with her jewellery and valuables for the marriage of her sister-in-law but the matter was not pressed further on her refusal and there was no harassment or coercion by her in-laws, it was held that it did not amount to cruelty.

Accused guilty of offence in any case; to hold an accused guilty of the offence under section 498-A of the Indian Penal Code, the prosecution is required to prove beyond reasonable doubt that the respondent was subjected to cruelty or harassment, by the accused. From the evidence of the prosecution witnesses and in particular witnesses, this Court finds that they have made general allegations of harassment by the petitioner towards the respondent 1 and have not brought in evidence any specific acts of cruelty or harassment by the petitioner on the respondent.

In the present case, although the learned Trial Court has found the petitioner guilty conduct and the Appellate Court has also upheld the same, but the cruelty as has been indicated under section 498-A of the Indian Penal Code is not at all proved

In Bathala Subbarayudu v. State of A.P.,

the bride was ill-treated and harassed by her in-laws for not bringing adequate dowry. On the day of occurrence, when her husband was away, she was abused and beaten by them and her father-in-law poured kerosene over her body and set fire to her clothes. She died in the hospital. On the basis of two consistent dying declarations of the deceased, the father in-law was convicted and sentenced under Sections 302 and 498-A.

In Balbir Singh v. State of Punjab,

The Supreme Court held that in view of the fact that victim was rescued by neighbour case of suicide must be ruled out and the conviction Of accused under Section 302, IPC was held proper. However, conviction of both the accused under Section 498-A was held proper.

CHAPTER 21 - OF DEFAMATION [499 TO 502]

Section 499. Defamation. –

Whoever, by words, either spoken or intended to be read, or by signs or by visible representations, makes or publishes any imputation concerning any person, intending to harm, or knowing or having reason to believe that such imputation will harm, the reputation of such person, is said, except in the cases hereinafter excepted, to defame that person.

Explanation I. - it may amount to defamation to impute anything to a deceased person, if the imputation would harm the reputation of that person if living, and is intended to be hurtful to the feelings of his family or other near relatives.

Explanation 2. -It may amount to defamation to make an imputation concerning a company or an association or collection of persons as such.

Explanation 3. -An imputation in the form of an alternative or expressed ironically may amount to defamation.

Explanation 4. -No imputation is said to harm a person's reputation, unless that imputation directly or indirectly, in the estimation of others, lowers the moral or intellectual character of that person, or lowers the character of that person in respect of his

caste or of his calling, or lowers the credit of that person or causes it to be believed that the body of that person is in a loathsome state, or in a state generally considered as disgraceful.

EXCEPTIONS.

(1) It is not defamation to impute anything which is true concerning any person, if it be for the public good that the imputation should be made or published. Whether or not it is for the public good is a question of fact.

(2) It is not defamation to express in good faith any opinion whatever respecting the conduct of a public servant in the discharge of his public functions, or respecting his character, so far as his character appears in that conduct, and no further.

(3) It is not defamation to express in good faith any opinion whatever respecting the conduct of any person touching any public question, and respecting his character, so far as his character appears in the conduct, and no further.

(4) It is not defamation to publish a substantially true report of the proceedings of a Court of Justice, or of the results of any such proceedings.

(5) It is not defamation to express in good faith any opinion whatever respecting the merits of any case, civil or criminal, which has been decided by a Court of Justice, or respecting the conduct of any person as a party, witness or agent, in any such case, or respecting the character of such person, as far as his character appears in that conduct, and no further.

(6) It is not defamation to express in good faith any opinion respecting the merits of any performance which its author has submitted to the judgment of the public or respecting the character of the author so far as his character appears in such performance, and no further.

(7) It is not defamation in a person having over another any authority, either conferred by law or arising out of a lawful contract made with that other, to pass in good faith any censure

on the conduct of that other in matters to which such lawful authority relates.

(8) It is not defamation to prefer in good faith an accusation against any person to any of those who have lawful authority over that person with respect to the subject-matter of accusation.

(9) It is not defamation to make an imputation on the character of another provided that the imputation be made in good faith for the protection of the interest of the person making it, or of any other person, or for the public good.

(10) It is not defamation to convey a caution, in good faith to one person against another, provided that such caution be intended for the good of the person to whom it is conveyed, or of some person in whom that person is interested, or for the public good.

Section 500. Punishment for defamation. -

Whoever defames another shall be punished with simple imprisonment for a term which may extend to 2 years, or with or with both.

ESSENTIAL INGREDIENTS

(1) Making or publishing any imputation concerning any person;

(2) Such imputation must have been made by -

    (a) Words, either spoken or intended to be read, or

    (b) signs, or

    (c) Visible representations;

(3) Such imputation must have been made with the intention of harming or with knowledge or reason to

believe that it will harm the reputation of the person concerning whom it is made.

(1) Makes or publishes any imputation. -

Every person who composes, dictates, writes or in any way contributes to the making of a libel is the maker of the libel. Where 'the matter is dictated by one person and written down by another person, both shall be guilty of this offence. Similarly, if one person speaks, another writes and third approves of it, all the three shall be guilty.

Publishes. -The defamatory matter must be published that is, communication of the defamatory matter to some person other than the person about whom it is addressed. Communicating defamatory matter only to the person defamed is not publication.

In P.R. Ramkrishnan v. Subbramma, where the complainant's advocate sent a notice to a party whose advocate dictated a reply to his steno containing defamatory remarks and the same was sent to the complainant's advocate the Kerala High Court held that this did not amount to any publication.

Defamatory matter, if written on a postcard, or printed on a paper will constitute publication when it is distributed or broadcasted.

If a defamatory letter against wife is sent to the husband or vice-versa, such a communication will constitute publication, but uttering of libel by a husband to his wife or by wife to husband would not constitute publication because they are regarded as one in the eye of law.

Sale of each copy of a printed libel is a distinct publication of a fresh offence and hence the accused will be punished for publishing several copies.

The publisher of a libel is strictly responsible, irrespective of the fact whether he is the originator of the libel or is merely repeating it.

Imputation. - it is necessary that the words should contain imputation concerning some specific person or persons whose identity can be established. It may concern to an individual or a class of individuals. The imputation may be conveyed obliquely or indirectly, or by way of question, conjecture, exclamation or by irony.

(2) Imputation should have been made by words either spoken or intended to be read, or by signs or by visible representation. -

The Indian and English law differs on this point. In English law, words are defamatory only when it is in writing, printing, engraving or some similar process. In India, a person can be defamed not only by writings, but he can also be defamed by spoken words. In it the term 'defamation' is used to embrace both libel and slander.

The words 'visible representation' will include every possible form of defamation which ingenuity can devise, e.g., a statute, a caricature, an effigy, chalk marks on a wall, signs, or pictures may constitute a libel.

(3) Intending to harm, or knowing or having reason to believe that such imputation will harm. -

The expression 'harm' means harm to the reputation of the aggrieved party. It is not necessary to prove that the complainant actually suffered directly or indirectly from the scandalous imputation alleged, it is sufficient to show that the accused intended to harm, or 'knew, or has reason to believe that the imputation made by him would harm the reputation of the complainant.

The test to determine whether any statement is defamatory or not is whether under the circumstances in which writing was published, a person of reasonable prudence to whom publication was made be likely to understand it in a libellous sense. By 'harm, is meant imputation on a man's character made and expressed to others so as to lower him in their estimation. Anything which lowers him in his own estimation does not constitute defamation.

In M.P Narayana Pillai and others v. M.P. Chako and another, the Court held that where an article is published in many parts and some containing defamatory materials, others not, in such a case the article as a whole must be read. The impact and effect of the imputations has to be considered in the background of the entire facts and circumstances stated therein. If the disreputable part can be removed by the other parts and the conclusions, then no prosecution for defamation can be launched by picking and choosing the disreputable part alone. The circumstances under which and the portions of the article wherein the alleged defamatory imputations occur and their impact on the mind of the reader or reading the article as a whole has to be considered.

Section 501. Printing or engraving matter known to be defamatory. -

Whoever prints or engraves any matter knowing or having good reasons to believe that such matter is defamatory of any person, shall be punished with simple imprisonment for a term which may extend to 2 years or with fine or with both.

Section 502. Sale of printed or engraved substance containing defamatory matter. -
Whoever sells or offers for sale any printed or engraved substance containing defamatory matter, knowing that it contains such matter, shall be punished with simple imprisonment for a term which may extend to 2 years or with fine or with both.

CHAPTER 22 - OF CRIMINAL INTIMIDATION, INSULT AND ANNOYANCE [503 TO 511]

Section 503: Criminal Intimidation. –

Whoever threatens another with an injury to his person, reputation or property, or to the person or reputation of any one in whom that person is interested, with intent to cause alarm to that person, or to cause that person to do any act which he is not legally bound to do, or to omit to do any act which that person is legally entitled to do, as a means of avoiding the execution of such threat, commits criminal intimidation.

Explanation. -Ä threats to injure the reputation of any deceased person in whom the person threatened is interested, is within this section.

ESSENTIAL INGREDIENTS

(1) Threatening a person with an injury -
    (1) To his person, reputation, or property, or
    (2) To his person, or reputation of any one in whom that person is interested.
(2) The threat must be with intent -
    (1) To cause alarm to that person, or

(2) To cause that person to do any act which he is not legally bound to do as a means of avoiding the execution of such threat, or

(3) To cause that person to omit to do any act which that person is legally

entitled to do as a means of avoiding the execution of such threat.

The gist of the offence under Section 503 lies in the effect which the threat is intended

to have upon the mind of the person threatened and it is clear that before it can have any effect upon his mind it must be either made to him by the person threatening or communicated to him in some way.

In Purshotam Vanamali, a constable was sent to fetch to a police Inspector some persons from whom the latter wished to make inquiries regarding an offence. While the constable was taking two people with him, the accused came up and threatened them both and the constable with the head constable's vengeance, and as a consequence the two persons refused to accompany the constable who had to go without them. It was held that the accused were guilty of the offence under Section 503.

Section 506. Punishment for criminal intimidation. –

Whoever commits the offence of criminal intimidation shall be punished with imprisonment of either description for a term which may extend to 2 years, or with fine or with both; and if the threat be to cause death or grievous hurt or to cause the destruction of any property by fire, or to cause an offence punishable with death or imprisonment for life or with imprisonment for a term which may extend to 7 years or to impute unchastity to a woman, shall be punishable with imprisonment of either description for a term which may extend to 7 years, or with fine, or with both.

Section 504. -Intentional insult with intent to provoke breach of the peace. -

Whoever intentionally insults, and thereby gives provocation to any person, intending or knowing it to be likely that such provocation will cause him to break the public peace, or to commit any other offence, shall be punished with imprisonment of either description for a term which may extend to 2 years, or with fine, or with both.

ESSENTIAL INGREDIENTS

(1) Intentionally insulting a person and thereby giving provocation to him; and

(2) The person insulting must intend or know it to be likely that such provocation will cause him to break the public peace or to commit any other offence.

Section 505. -Statements conducing to public mischief. –

(1) Whoever makes, publishes or circulates any statement, rumour or report, -

> (a) with intent to cause, or which is likely to cause, any officer, soldier, sailor or
> Airman in the Army, Navy or Air Force of India to mutiny or otherwise disregard or fail in his duty as such; or
>
> (b) with intent to cause, or which is likely to cause, fear or alarm to the public, or to any section of the public whereby any person may be induced to commit an

offence against the State or against the public tranquillity; or

(c) with intent to incite, or which is likely to incite any class or community of persons to commit any offence against any other class or community, shall be punished with imprisonment which may extend to 3 years, or with fine or with both.

(2) Statement creating or promoting enmity, hatred or ill will between classes. -Whoever, makes, publishes or circulates any statement or report containing rumour or alarming news with intent to create or promote, or which is likely to create or promote, on grounds of religion, race, place of birth, residence, language, caste or community or any other ground whatsoever, feelings of enmity, hatred or ill-will between different religious, racial, language or regional groups or castes or communities shall be punished with imprisonment which may extend to 3 years, or with fine, or with both.

(3) Offence under sub-section (2) committed in place of worship, etc. - commits an offence specified in sub-section (2) in any place of worship or in any assembly engaged in the performance of religious worship or religious ceremonies, shall be punished with imprisonment which may extend to 5 years and shall also be liable to fine.

Exception. -

it does not amount to an offence, within the meaning of this section, when the person making, publishing or circulating any such statement, rumour or report, has reasonable grounds for believing that such statement, rumour or report is true and makes, publishes or circulates it in good faith and without any such intent as aforesaid.

Section 507. Criminal intimidation by an anonymous communication. -

Whoever commits the offence of criminal intimidation by an anonymous communication, or having taken precautions to conceal the name or abode of the person from whom the threat comes, shall be punished with imprisonment of either description for a term which may extend to 2 years, in addition to the punishment provided for the offence by the last preceding section.

Section 508. Act caused by inducing person to believe that he will be rendered an object of divine displeasure. -Whoever voluntarily causes or attempts to cause any person to do anything which that person is not legally bound to do, or to omit to do anything which he is legally entitled to do, by inducing or attempting to induce that person to believe that he or any person in whom he is interested will be rendered by some act of the offender an object of Divine displeasure if he does not do the thing which it is the object of the offender to cause him to do or if he does the thing which it is the object of the offender to cause him to omit, shall be punished with imprisonment of either description for a term which may extend to one year, or with fine, or with both.

Section 509. Word, gesture or act intended to insult the modesty of a woman. –

Whoever, intending to insult the modesty of any woman, utters any word, makes any sound or gesture, or exhibits any object, intending that such word or sound shall be heard, or that such gesture or object shall be seen, by such woman, or intrudes upon the privacy of such woman, [shall be punished with simple imprisonment for a term which may extend to three years, and also with fine.]

ESSENTIAL INGREDIENTS

(1) Intention to insult the modesty of a woman;
(2) The insult must be caused -
(a) by uttering any word or making any sound or gesture or exhibiting any object intending that such word or sound shall be heard, or that such gesture or object shall be seen, by such woman, or
(b) by intruding upon the privacy of such woman.

In Tarah Das Gupta, the accused a University graduate, wrote a letter containing indecent overtures and posted it in an envelope addressed to an English nurse with whom he was not acquainted. It was held that the accused intended to insult the modesty of the nurse and that the letter, though enclosed in an envelope, was an object which was exhibited to the nurse to whose address it was posted.

Section 510: Misconduct in public by a drunken person. –

Whoever, in a state of intoxication, appears in any public place, or in any place which it is a trespass in him to enter and there conducts himself in such a manner as to cause annoyance to any person shall be punished with simple imprisonment for a term which may extend to twenty-four hours, or with fine which may extend to ten rupees or with both.

ESSENTIAL INGREDIENTS

(1) Appearance of a person in a state of intoxication in –
(a) any public place; or
(b) any place which it is trespass in him to enter.
(2) The person so appearing must have conducted himself in such a manner as to cause annoyance to any person.

CHAPTER 23 - OF ATTEMPTS TO COMMIT OFFENCES

Section 511. Punishment for attempting to commit offences punishable with imprisonment for life or other imprisonment. –

Whoever, attempts to commit an offence punishable by this Code with imprisonment for life or imprisonment or to cause such an offence to be committed, and in such attempt does any act towards the commission of the offence, shall, where no express provision is made by this Code for the Punishment of such attempt, be punished with imprisonment of any description provided for the offence, for a term which may extend to one-half of imprisonment for life or, as the case may be, one-half of the longest term of imprisonment provided for that offence, or with such fine as is provided for the offence, or with both.

Attempt is one of the four stages in the commission of a crime. The first is intention, which is not punishable by itself. The second stage is preparation which is also not ordinarily punishable. Attempt is the third stage. In the attempt to commit a crime, it is punishable. The last stage is commission of the crime. This is also punishable.

In Reg v. Eagleton,

ATTEMPT IS DEFINED:

"The mere intention to commit a misdemeanour is not criminal. Some act is required, and we do not think that all acts towards committing a misdemeanour indictable. Acts remotely leading towards the commission of the offence, are not to be considered as attempts to commit but acts immediately connected with it are..."

The test of proximity stated in this case has been accepted and applied.

Difference between preparation and attempt. -The border line between preparation and attempt is very thin and sometimes, what one considers to be an attempt, turns out to be mere preparation. R. V. Robinson provides a good illustration. P, a jeweller, with the object of fraudulently obtaining insurance money, removed the stock of his jewellery from the safe to another place, left the safe open, tied himself up beneath a chain and called aloud for help. A police man hearing the shouts, entered the house. P narrates his "story" to the policeman. Subsequently, investigations showed that this was all a drama enacted by P to defraud the insurance company. The Court held that P could not be convicted of an attempt to obtain money by false pretences, as his act had been merely an act of preparation for the crime and not a step towards it.

In Aman Kumar v. State of Haryana, it was held by the Supreme Court that the word attempt is to be understood in its ordinary meaning. It has to be distinguished from intention to commit offence and preparation. Attempt means an act which if not prevented would have resulted in full consummation of act attempted.

In Haughton v. Smith, certain goods were stolen from a firm in X. Some days later, a van, travelling south, was stopped by the police. It contained stolen goods. It was revealed that the van was proceeding to a place where accused was to make an arrangement for the disposal of goods. In order to trap the accused, the van was allowed to proceed to its destination with two policemen concealed in the van and one sitting by the side of the driver, in disguise. At the destination, accused along with another person, actively engaged himself in unloading the van. At this stage, the trap was sprung up and, the accused and other persons were apprehended. The accused was charged with attempt to handle stolen goods. He was acquitted. The Court held that:

"A person commits the offence of "attempt to commit a particular offence" when -

(1) he intends to commit that particular offence; and

(2) he having made preparations and with the intention to commit the offence, does an act towards its commission, such an act need not be penultimate act towards the commission of offence but must be an act during the course of

In Bashir Bhai v. State of Bombay, the Supreme Court said that persons, who were caught in a trap as a result of the complainant acting in consort with' the police. One guilty of the offence of attempt at cheating. In this case, the accused represented to the complainant that he could duplicate the notes. The complainant pretending to believe the accused, handed over to him some currency notes after consulting police. The police apprehended the accused in the very act of handing over the notes along with the material of duplicate.

PROBLEMS AND SOLUTIONS

1.

'A' a surgeon in good faith communicates to 'B' a patient his opinion that he cannot survive. The patient dies in consequence of shock.

Ans. - instant problem is based on Section 93 of IPC which provides that no communication made in good faith is an offence by reason of any harm to the person to whom it is made, if it is made for the benefit of that person.

In the above problem, a communication made to the patient by the surgeon is in good faith as such no offence has been committed by the surgeon although the patient dies due to such communication. Thus, the surgeon is protected under this section.

2.

'A' intended to steal an umbrella from a club of which he was a member. He opened the closet, '-used an umbrella was his own which he had lost a weak earlier. Discuss whether 'A' has committed any offence?

Ans. -In the above problem, A is neither liable for theft nor for attempting to commit theft because a person cannot be convicted of stealing his own property if it does not take it dishonestly from another. In this problem, A has neither taken any wrongful gain nor cause any wrongful loss to any person, since the umbrella was his 01.vn which he had lost a week earlier. In this way, A has committed no offence as defined under the Indian Penal Code.

3.

'X' gave a kick to 'Y, who had an enlarged spleen. As a result of the kick, the spleen was ruptured and 'Y died. Giving reason, state what offence had been committed?

Ans.-Present problem is based on Munnilal's case, wherein the accused person sat on the chest of another person and began to strangle him and did not desist despite intervention by his relatives. That person died due to internal bleeding on account of rupture of the spleen which was enlarged already. It was shown that the other injuries of the victims were not sufficient to cause death had the spleen not been ruptured. The fact of the spleen being not known to the accused person. Hence, the accused person was held guilty of culpable homicide not amounting to murder under second part of Section 304.

From the above decision it is clear that in the given problem, 'X' is guilty of culpable homicide not amounting to murder under second part of Section 304.

4.

State with reasons what offence, if any, has been committed:

'A' is in a house which is in fire with Z' a child, People below hold out a blanket, 'A' drops the child from the housetop, knowing it to be likely that the fall may kill the child, but not intending to kill the child and in good faith for the child's benefit. The child is killed by the fall.

Ans.-Present problem is based on illustration (d) of Section 92 of IPC, 1860. According to which, "A is in a house x, which is on fire, with Z, a child. People below hold out a blanket. 'A' drops the child from the house top, knowing it to be likely that the fall may kill the child, but not intending to kill the child and intending in good faith, the child's benefit. Hence even if the child is killed by the fall, A has committed no offence." Hence in this problem A has committed no offence.

5.

'A' a surgeon, in good faith, communicates to a patient, his opinion that he cannot survive. The patient dies in consequence of the shock.

Ans.-Present problem is based on the illustration of Section 93 of IPC. 1860. According to which, A, a surgeon, in good faith communicates to a patient his opinion that he cannot live. The patient dies in consequence of shock. A has committed no offence, though he knew it to be likely that the communication might cause the patient's death. Hence, in this problem, 'A', a surgeon has committed no offence.

6.

'A instigates 'B' to murder 'D'. 'B' stabs 'D'. 'D' recovers from the wound. What offence 'A' and 'B' have committed? Discuss

Ans. -The given problem is based on the illustration (b) of the explanation 2 of Section 108 of the Indian Penal Code, 1860. 'A' according to which A instigates B to murder C. B. in pursuance of the instigation stabs D. D recovers from the wound. A is guilty of instigating B to commit murder.

Hence, in the present problem, 'A' is guilty of instigating 'B' to commit murder of 'D' and 'B' may be guilty of grievous hurt, or attempt to commit murder, as the case may be.

7.

'A' cuts down a tree on B's ground with the intention of dishonestly taking the tree from B's possession without B's consent.

Ans. -In the instant problem, A is liable for theft under Section 379, IPC as the tree has become movable property, the moment it was cut down. Section 379, IPC provides that taking dishonestly movable property from another's possession without his consent constitutes theft. So, here 'A' is liable for committing theft under Section 379, IPC

8.

'A' attempts to pull 'Z's nose, 'Z' in the exercise of the right of private defence, lays hold of 'A' to prevent him from doing so. 'A' is moved to sudden and violent passion in consequence and kills 'Z'. [U.P. PCS 2015]

Ans. -Present problem is based on illustration (e) of Section 300 of I.P.C., 1860.

According to which, "A attempts to pull Z's nose. Z, in the exercise of the right of private defence, lays hold of A to prevent him from doing so. A is moved to sudden and violent passion in consequence and kills Z. This is murder, inasmuch as the provocation was given by a thing in the exercise of the right of private defence." Hence in this problem A committed murder of Z.

9.

A instigates B to burn C's house. B sets fire to the house and at the same time commits theft of property there. What offence A and B have committed? Discuss.

Ans. -In the above problem, A is guilty of abetting the burning of the house only and in not abetting the theft because the theft was a distinct and separate act which is not a probable consequence of the burning. The present problem is based on the illustration (b) of Section 111 of the IPC

In the above case, A has instigated B only to burn Cs house and not for committing theft of property there. Theft of property is a different act and which cannot be attributed a probable consequence of the burning. So, A has committed the offence of abetting of the burning of house only. B has also committed the offence of theft as defined under Section 378, IPC

10.

A instigates B to give false evidence. B does not give false evidence. Has committed any offence? Discuss. V.P. PCS (J), 2003]

Ans. -Present problem is based on illustration (a) of explanation 2 of Section 108 of the Indian Penal Code, 1860 according to which, A instigates B to murder C. B refuses to do so. A is guilty of abetting B to commit murder.

Hence, in the given problem, A instigates B to give false evidence, but B does not give false evidence, A is guilty of abetting B to give false evidence.

11.

A enters B's house in the night with the intention of committing theft but moved by B's poverty drops a 500 rupee note and comes back.

Ans. -In the above problem, A is liable for committing criminal trespass under Section 441, IPC as well as for attempting to commit theft under Section 379 read with Section 511, IPC

12.

A 13 years old girl went to see a fete with her maternal uncle. Due to heavy crowd in fete, she became separated from her maternal uncle. She could not remember even address of her house. One person enticed her to go to his house and took her away to his house. There at his residence he prepared for the marriage of this girl with his son. In the meantime, this person was arrested by police. Will he be convicted for kidnapping? Answer with reason.

Ans. -In the above problem, that person has committed the offence of kidnapping under Section 363, IPC because kidnapping from lawful guardianship is an offence under Section 361 1.P.C

Explanation of Section 361, IPC provides that lawful guardian includes any person lawfully entrusted with the care or custody of such minor or other person. In the present case maternal uncle of girl is her lawful guardian at that time also '. when she was separated from her maternal uncle. As such the person has committed the offence of kidnapping under Section 363, IPC

13.

"A", finds a valuable ring on the road. He picks it up and sells it immediately. What offence has been committed by "A"?

Ans. -In this problem, "an' is guilty of an offence of dishonest misappropriation of property under Section 403 of IPC, because "A" sells the ring immediately without attempting to discover the owner.

14.

flew away with an airplane without permission of the authorities. However, he restored the airplane at its place a day after.

Ans. — In the present problem, A has committed the offence of theft under Section 379, I.P.C. because in the commission of the offence of the theft it is not necessary that the taking must be permanent or with an intention to appropriate the thing taken. In other words, if a person takes away any movable property out of the possession of another person even though temporarily and with an intention to return it later on, it would amount to theft. The present problem is based on the case of Pyarelal.

15.

The Chief Minister of a State asked an industrialist to donate rupees ten lac to his party fund, otherwise his licence shall be cancelled. Industrialist quietly gave the desired amount to his political party. [U.P. PCS (J), 19991

Ans.—In the present problem, Chief Minister has not committed an offence under Section 383 of I.P.C. because there is no evidence at all that industrialist has donated rupees ten lacs after being put in any fear and the amount had been paid in response to threats. Thus, the Chief Minister has not extorted the industrialist as such no offence of extortion has been committed by him.

16.

'A' intentionally pulls up a woman's veil without her consent. Whether any offence has been committed by A?

Ans.—In the present problem, A has used criminal force to her as such A has committed the offence of criminal force under Section 350, I.P.C. because here A has intentionally and without the consent of the women and intending or knowing it to be likely that he may thereby injure, frighten or annoy her by pulling up her veil. And thus, A is liable for the offence of criminal force.

17.

A and B were two joint owners of a shop. A put his lock on the shop which was let out by B the other joint owner without A's consent. The tenant made a complaint against A. What offence, if any, has been committed by A?

Ans. — In the instant problem, no offence has been committed by A because A has put his lock to a house of which he was the joint owner, and the complainant was his tenant.

18.

A, an officer of a court of justice, being ordered by that court to arrest Y, and after due enquiry, believing Z to be Y, arrests Z. What an offence has been committed by

Ans.—In the present case, A has committed no offence and he is entitled to get the benefit of Section 76 of I.P.C. because A was bound by law to follow the order given by the court and A arrests Z by a mistake of fact. Therefore, no offence has been committed by A.

19.

A student leader of University declared himself for self-immolation. He got logs piled up in front of the main gate of the University and sprinkled kerosene oil over it. Thereafter he climbed over the pile of wood and sprinkled kerosene oil upon himself too. In the meantime, police came and registered a case of "attempt to commit suicide". Answer, giving reason whether the student is guilty of committing the said offence.

Ans. — In the given problem, student leader of a University declared himself for self-immolation. He got logs up in front of the main gate of the University and sprinkled kerosene oil over it. Thereafter he climbed over the pile of wood and sprinkled kerosene oil upon himself too. In the meantime, police came there, caught him and registered a case for committing a case of "attempt to commit suicide."

In the present problem, he will not be liable for attempt to commit suicide as his act is said to be only preparation and not attempt to commit suicide and there was sufficient possibility to alter his mind before lighting the match for self-immolation. But if he had
been caught by the police just after striking a match to it or after lighting match or during burning condition, he would be guilty of attempt to commit suicide.

20.

'A' puts jewels into a box belonging to 'Z' with the intention that they may be found in that box and the circumstance may-cause 'Z' to be convicted of theft.

Ans. -Present problem is based on illustration of Section 378 of IPC, 1860. According to which, "A finds a ring belonging to Z on a table in the house which Z occupies. Here the ring is in Z's possession and if A dishonestly removes it, A commits theft."

Hence in this problem, 'A' puts jewels into a box belonging to 'Z' with the intention that they may be found in that box and this circumstance may cause 'Z' to be convicted of theft, then it is clear that A dishonestly puts jewels into a box belonging to Z and therefore, 'A' has committed theft.

21.

'A' is the paramour of 'Z's wife. She gives a valuable property to A which A knows that it belongs to her husband Z and as such she has no authority from 'Z' to give it to A. Inspite of this 'A' takes the property. Whether 'A' has committed any offence? If yes, what offence?

Ans. -Present problem is based on illustrations (o) of Section 378 of the IPC, 1860. According to which "A is the paramour of 'Z's wife. She gives a valuable property, which A knows to belong to her husband Z, and to be such property as she has no authority from Z to give. If A takes the property dishonestly. He commits theft."

Hence, in this problem, since 'A' takes the property in spite of knowing it very well that the property was of husband Z and for which wife of Z has no authority to give that property to any person, hence 'A' has committed theft and he is guilty under this section

22.

'A' finds a valuable ring, not knowing to whom it belongs. 'A' sells it immediately without attempting to discover the owner. Whether A has committed any offence? If yes, what offence?

Ans.-Present problem is based on illustrations (f) of Section 403 of the IPC, 1860. According to which "A finds a valuable ring, not knowing to whom it belongs. 'A' sells it immediately without attempting to discover the owner. A is guilty of an offence under this section.

Hence in this problem A has committed dishonest misappropriation of property and he is guilty under this section.

23.

'A' being on friendly terms with 'Y goes into 'y's in Y's absence and takes away a book without Y's express consent for the purpose merely of reading it and with the intention of returning it and with the intention of returning it to his friend.

Ans. -Present problem is based on the illustration (m) of Section 378 of the Indian Penal Code, According to which A, being on friendly terms with Z, goes into Z's in Z's absence, and takes away a book without Z's express consent for the purpose of merely reading it, and with the intention of returning it. Here, it is probable that A may have conceived that he had Z's implied consent to use Z's book If this was A's intention. A has not committed theft. -Hence, in this problem if the intention of A is that he had Y's implied consent to use Y's book, then A has not committed theft otherwise, he has committed theft.

www.ingramcontent.com/pod-product-compliance
Lightning Source LLC
Chambersburg PA
CBHW071448220526
45472CB00003B/711